Every time I see a positive work on Hagar and
Christian pen, I rejoice and feel encouraged th
redeeming love outside the line of Promise is b
Finding Hagar mixes in a beautiful way both se
applications. The corporate effort behind this work involving
pictures drawn by his daughter points to the cordiality and passion with which
this work was done. I wholeheartedly recommend this beautiful, serious and
yet simple, work by Kuhn to every student of the Bible and especially to every
Christian worker in the Arab World.

Tony Maalouf, PhD
Distinguished Professor of World Christianity and Middle Eastern Studies,
Southwestern Baptist Theological Seminary, Fort Worth, Texas, USA
Visiting Professor,
Jordan Evangelical Theological Seminary, Amman, Jordan

Finding Hagar takes on itself the task of gently – and persuasively! – adjusting
any misconceptions we might have on the place of Ishmael in God's larger
scheme. By dovetailing the biblical narratives in Genesis with Jewish and Islamic
traditions, Kuhn provides a panoramic timeline on which readers can travel
up and down, revisiting familiar places and people and meeting new pieces
of information. The encounters require that we rethink our presuppositions.
And they challenge us to take our place in the continuing story of Hagar and
her children.

Havilah Dharamraj, PhD
Academic Dean and Head, Department of Old Testament,
South Asia Institute of Advanced Christian Studies, Bangalore, India

Mike Kuhn's book on Hagar and Ishmael will open your eyes to what has been
hidden in the shadows and has been overlooked. In this book, the spotlight
is shed on Hagar as one of the best supporting actors in God's drama of
redemptive history. Does Hagar speak to us today? In this book you will see
how she speaks to us and to our burning issues. I wish every Christian would
read this book as it brings grace to two irritant and misunderstood figures,
Hagar and Ishmael. Once I started reading this book, I could not stop until I
finished it.

Nabeel T. Jabbour, ThD
Author, *The Crescent through the Eyes of the Cross*

As one who has had the Middle East as his assignment from the heart of God for over fifty years, I was captivated by this page-turning entrance into the Patriarch Abraham's country in the light of Mike Kuhn's artistic insights. This amazingly accomplished Arabist and scholar, with his wife, Stephanie, have absorbed a depth of understanding of the nuances of Middle East culture, with historical biblical insights, so that the reader is transported into Hagar's life . . . brought to life as you've never known it before! The bonus is that you'll want to read your Old Testament with fresh depth and enjoyment.

Greg Livingstone
Founder, Frontiers

Hagar, the first female theologian, and her firstborn son, Ishmael, circumcised under the Abraham covenant, is the story retold born out of Kuhn's decades of living in Middle Eastern society. He brings a wider vision and biblical scholarship to this story that has been misunderstood by Christians throughout history. A blessing at the time, now interpreted in the modern mind as a curse with tragic repercussions for millions of people. By retelling this ancient saga, we are having our own prejudices revealed. A must-read.

Christine A. Mallouhi
Author, *Waging Peace on Islam* and *Miniskirts, Mothers and Muslims*

Few Christians understand the depth of emotional feelings that Muslims attach to their perceived lineage through Hagar and Ishmael. Mike Kuhn expertly weaves his personal experiences with Arabs along with significant research to break new ground for the reader seeking to plumb the mindset, not only of Arabs, but also of Muslims worldwide. Particularly helpful are Kuhn's extrapolations from Hagar to oppressed migrants in our contemporary settings.
 Kudos on a job well done.

Phil Parshall, DMiss
Author, *Lifting the Veil* and *The Cross and the Crescent*
Retired, SIM USA

Finding Hagar

Langham
GLOBAL LIBRARY

Finding Hagar

God's Pursuit of a Runaway

Michael F. Kuhn

Illustrated by Bethany Giles

Langham
GLOBAL LIBRARY

Text © 2019 Michael F. Kuhn

Published 2019 by Langham Global Library
An imprint of Langham Publishing
www.langhampublishing.org

Langham Publishing and its imprints are a ministry of Langham Partnership

Langham Partnership
PO Box 296, Carlisle, Cumbria, CA3 9WZ, UK
www.langham.org

ISBNs:
978-1-78368-647-6 Print
978-1-78368-653-7 ePub
978-1-78368-654-4 Mobi
978-1-78368-655-1 PDF

British Library Cataloguing-in-Publication Data
A catalogue record for this book is available from the British Library

ISBN: 978-178368-647-6

Illustrations: © Bethany Giles
Cover & Book Design: projectluz.com

To Stephanie
A cherished companion on the journey

CONTENTS

Preface

Reconsidering an Old Story

I used to read quickly over the Hagar story, mostly to confirm my own suspicions, which I now recognize as dangerous biases. I had no doubt that her son Ishmael was destined to enmity and isolation. I could see in the Hagar story the embryo of present-day geopolitical conflicts in the Middle East.

"Way leads on to way," as Robert Frost says, and I ended up spending nearly half my life in the Middle East. Over many years, I came to love Middle Eastern people, their culture, and their language. I also began to see Hagar in a new light.

In the pages that follow, I invite you to join me on that journey.

Disclosure: Part of this story is my imagination, inspired by the culture and social life of the Middle East. I have grounded it all in the biblical text and put it together in such a way that you will know when the text is speaking and when my imagination takes over.

Through it all, I ask you to consider a different perspective – that Hagar represents many others in the long narrative of the Bible who fall outside the line of God's chosen people but who, nonetheless, were overwhelmed and rescued by a God whose goodness and grace pursued them to the ends of the earth.

Those characters include Jethro the pagan priest (father-in-law of Moses), Rahab the whore, Ruth the young Moabite widow, Job the son of the East, Nebuchadnezzar the idol-worshiping emperor, the Roman army captain, the Canaanite beggar woman, the Samaritan community represented by a woman who had given up on the institution of marriage, Luke the evangelist, a prison guard in Philippi, Onesimus the slave – and the list goes on until it reaches and includes you and me.

Understood properly, Hagar is not setting us up for a future of wars in the Middle East. On the contrary, she confronts us with a God whose grace is scandalous, whose love is profligate, and who pursues the fugitive until he finds her.

I hope you can be persuaded, but if you are like me, it may take a while. Be patient and ponder.

Allow me to introduce you to Hagar, the slave girl of Sarah.

Mike Kuhn

1

Shifha Sarai

*Now Sarai, Abram's wife, had borne him no
children. She had a female Egyptian servant
whose name was Hagar. (Genesis 16:1)*

I'm not sure why I'm here. The last thing I remember is running and playing around the threshing floor with the other children. The men were just finishing the day's work – bringing up the cattle after watering them down by the Nile.

Someone was visiting. They always honored the guests with a lot of food. A goat was slaughtered. Momma was cooking. She said I could come back later to help carry in the food.

When I went back, Momma was crying. I had no idea why. Her face was all red and wrinkled and wet with sweat and tears. She just looked at me. Then she wailed. I had heard her wail before, but never like this. She turned her eyes away, then buried her head in her shawl.

"Momma! Momma!"

A strong arm grabbed me around my waist and whisked me into the big tent. Our masters were sitting with the honored guests. The food was already presented. I was set down in front of them – as if I were food, too!

They looked me over and talked. I couldn't understand what they were saying. I had never heard talk like that. Are they talking about me? Why are they looking at me like that? What are they saying? What's happening?

Then the same arm grabbed me again. Soon I was sitting on the wagon which had brought the guests. I could still hear Momma's wailing, but only distantly.

The man growled, "Just sit here and be quiet. Don't make a sound."

So that's what I did.
Since that day, I'm Shifha Sarai – Sarah's slave girl.
I never saw Momma again.

The restricted horizon of the slave is unfathomable to those of us who have never known anything other than freedom and mobility. The body of the slave becomes the implement of another's will. The slave has no menu of options in the use of her time, for it is solely at the disposal of her possessor. The will is usurped and forced until it loses all resilience. Intellect can develop no further than the point of its usefulness to the slave owner. Any point beyond that is insubordination, mutiny in the making.

The story of Hagar is a story of slavery. In our day it is sometimes called domestic servitude. The dynamics are very similar, and the modern expression can be equally oppressive. Since the ancients lacked the restraining effect of public scrutiny, honed by contemporary regulative principles such as the United Nations Declaration of Human Rights, slavery did not need to be concealed. It was common, an accepted way of life. Economies were ordered and regimes sustained by the practice of slavery.

The sojourn of the children of Israel in Egypt provides the slavery paradigm. Their lot was to build the royal cities of the pharaohs. When their presence was deemed a threat, more work was demanded, only this time without the provision of resources. If that were not enough, murder was legitimized. Only divine providence, working through the bravery of the midwives, spared the children of Jacob from annihilation. God's intervention through the exodus is the Old Testament paradigm of salvation, fulfilled and surpassed in the New Testament by the salvation effected by God's Son, whom he also called "out of Egypt" (Matt 2:15).

In our story, however, the shoe is on the other foot. The Egyptian is owned by Jacob's grandmother, the matriarch of the covenant people. Hagar is Sarai's slave girl. We have no idea if she was bought by Abram for Sarai or if she was given as a gift. Perhaps a clue is offered in the story of Abram's sojourn in Egypt.

Abram clearly impressed the Egyptians, and so did his wife Sarai, whom he falsely claimed was his sister. As a result, she was taken into the harem of the pharaoh, who treated Abram well. When the monarch discovered that she was actually Abram's wife, he restored her to him and then sent Abram away, laden with gifts the pharaoh had showered on him.

It is plausible that Hagar was given to Sarai during her time in the harem. We can only speculate since neither the Bible nor extrabiblical tradition is of much help. What is certain is that Hagar is Egyptian. Since Abram and Sarai sojourned there, it is reasonable to infer that Hagar became Sarai's slave girl during the sojourn in Egypt.

Her name "Hagar" has literary significance and may be a play on words. It is formed from a common Semitic root of three letters (h-g-r). The latter syllable is similar to the Hebrew *gar,* meaning "stranger" or "sojourner," a person who is removed from kith and kin – an unfortunate status in the ancient world as it usually derived from a crisis or undesirable social standing. The first syllable (*ha*) is also the Hebrew definite article "the." Literally, Hagar is "the stranger." Hagar becomes a biblical example of a foreigner, the first of many who were outside the covenant God made with Abram and yet sojourned among the people of the covenant.

The word is preserved in another Semitic language, Arabic, where it means "to flee." Muhammad's flight from Mecca to Medina is known as the *higra* or *hijra* – and the Muslim calendar is known as the *hijri* calendar as it dates from that flight.

Her name also recalls another Hebrew word – *garar,* meaning "to drag away." The resemblance is evocative as the slave girl's unfortunate lot in life had dragged her away from her homeland and family.

The reader should see Hagar's enslavement as a sign of future realities which had been revealed to Abram when the Lord appeared to him in a vision.[1] Hagar is not the only sojourner in the story and the reappearance of Egypt is a tantalizing pointer to the day when the roles will be reversed. After cleaving the animals in half, Abram fell into a deep sleep while the smoking pot and flaming torch embodying the divine presence passed between the pieces. Then Abram learned that his progeny would spend four hundred years of servitude in a foreign land before returning to their inheritance promised by God.

Hagar is the inverse. She is the Egyptian enslaved by the covenant people. Will she fare better than the Israelites in their enslavement? Will Abram's clan demonstrate nobler, more humane qualities than the Egyptians? Will the God of the covenant, who heard the cries of the Israelites, also attend to her cry? Will Hagar be delivered?

---

1. Genesis 15.

2

Barren

And Sarai said to Abram, "Behold now, the LORD has prevented me from bearing children. Go in to my servant; it may be that I shall obtain children by her." And Abram listened to the voice of Sarai. (Genesis 16:2)

Since the day we married, he and I have been waiting in vain. I'm not asking for the moon after all. It's only what's expected of me as the dutiful wife I've always tried to be to Abram. So many times I've pictured the scene in my mind, willing it to happen – the joy of seeing that gentle smile stretch across his wrinkled face as I would lay our son on Abram's waiting lap.

A son would be his entire life – his present and his future, our family and our wealth, his name before our neighbors and kin, and our only hope of stability in this life of endless wandering.

This one simple thing, the one thing I live and breathe for, has been denied me by God.

Abram shares his dreams with me, but lately it's been just too much for any woman to handle. I just don't understand the man any more. Maybe being deprived of this, his heart's desire, for so long is making him imagine things. Is he hearing voices? He says God has told him that he'll become a great nation. When we don't even have a son! It makes me feel so utterly useless, helpless, barren of hope.

It's unbelievable, but somehow this husband of mine is convinced that his descendants will become "as many as the stars" and bless all the other nations. Come back to the real world, Abram!

But my Abram has always been serious, devoted, hard-working. All our friends know that he's a man of great faith. One time he rescued our nephew by going to war with the neighboring tribal chiefs. And wouldn't you know it, my Abram wouldn't accept any of the spoils of war! He wanted everyone to know that he was dependent on his God – Yahweh – and him alone.

It's really not like him to dream silly dreams. I'm at the end of my rope.

There is a way though. Abram can still have an heir – only it won't be from my womb. The very thought of it pains me deeply, but it seems like the only way. I shudder at the idea – but for his sake, I've decided to go ahead with it.

Even in the contemporary Middle East, marriage is for procreation. Sons are the ultimate prize. They carry on the family name and secure the ownership of the family property. A couple who produce only female offspring face the ubiquitous appeal to "keep trying!" The woman who produces no heir may face divorce or polygamy. Procuring a son is the goal.

That's the contemporary world. The passage of time has loosened the stranglehold of this cultural expectation, but not much. The ancient world regarded the absence of a male heir as grounds for divorce, and even a sign of divine displeasure, thus consigning the sterile wife to a life of shame and ignominy.

God had commanded Adam and Eve to "be fruitful and multiply" (Gen 1:28). In later Jewish thought, the man was required to take action after a ten year period without conception. Some think this custom derives from Sarai and Abram having returned from Egypt to dwell in Canaan for a period of ten years before action was taken to rectify the unfortunate situation.[1]

The Bible has an abundance of infertility stories, most of which end with God's intervention to produce a child after long years of forbearance. The stories include Rebekah (Isaac's wife), Rachel (Jacob's wife), Manoah's wife (mother of Samson), Hannah (Elkanah's wife and mother of Samuel), Michal (David's wife), Elizabeth (Zachariah's wife and mother of John the Baptist).

The stories depict two stark realities – the women's existential struggle due to infertility and the fact that it is God who withholds the fruit of the womb. Sarai attributes her infertility to the action of Yahweh who has "walled her in" from having a child. Apparently male infertility was not considered a factor.

The psychological suffering that these women endured had ramifications for their marital relationship. Rachel's tormented cry to Jacob captures the angst: "Give me children, or I shall die!"[2] For some, the suffering drove them to new dependence on God as they pleaded with him for a child. Sarai's decision was no doubt borne out of great trauma and confusion. Something simply must be done. The family must survive and Abram must produce an heir.

Sarai is often censured for her action, and not without reason, for no less than the apostle Paul would subsequently refer to Hagar's offspring as "born according to the flesh."[3] We will consider Paul's allegory later. But the reality is that Sarai's conduct was noble according to the dictates of her culture and

---

1. Judith R. Baskin, "Infertile Wife in Rabbinic Judaism," *Jewish Women's Archive Encyclopedia*, 4 January 2019, https://jwa.org/encyclopedia/article/infertile-wife-in-rabbinic-judaism.

2. Genesis 30:1b.

3. Galatians 4:23a.

time.[4] The obvious course of action is never brought up by Abram, though the normal expectation was that he would act to rectify this unfortunate situation. Sarai has at her disposal the only acceptable solution. The slave girl can bear Abram's child. Sarai acts in the interest of her husband.

The suggestion that the slave girl bear Abram's child may offend the sensibilities of the contemporary reader. So be it. This story is set in ancient Canaan and accurately reflects the culture and customs of the time. The apparent harshness of the plot need not overly disturb us, for nowhere does the narrative claim to be prescriptive. It is descriptive, depicting God's intervention at a definite time and place, working in his providential care through the cultural values of the characters.

In fact, the siring of offspring through a slave was common in the ancient Near East. In an Assyrian marriage contract it is stipulated that if the wife fails to produce offspring within two years, she must purchase a slave for the purpose of bearing children. A similar practice is found in the ancient law code of Hammurabi, which makes provision for a childbearing slave for the husband of a priestess who is not allowed to bear children.[5]

The tone of the narrative, however, does not allow us to see this as a mere transaction. The lack of offspring had already been noted in Abram's deliberations with Yahweh in an earlier chapter: "O Lord GOD, what will you give me, for I continue childless, and the heir of my house is Eliezer of Damascus?"[6] If Isaac was born when Sarah was ninety, she would have been in her late seventies when she began to consider the possibility of Hagar bearing Abram's heir. At this stage of life, she has held out as long as possible, hoping against hope for conception. Now, however, hope is gone. Drastic measures are in order and Sarai comes forward with a plan to salvage the family honor.

One other point is worth noting. Though Abram had heard God's promise of a multitude of descendants, we have no record that those descendants were promised through Sarai. That happens only after he has had a son by Hagar: "No, but Sarah your wife shall bear you a son, and you shall call his name Isaac."[7] We may be less harsh in our judgment of Sarai when we realize that her body is well past childbearing years and she is acting for the sake of Abram's

4. Tony Maalouf, *Arabs in the Shadow of Israel: The Unfolding of God's Prophetic Plan for Ishmael's Line* (Grand Rapids, MI: Kregel, 2003), 51–53. See Maalouf for more Ancient Near Eastern background concerning the practice of obtaining children through slaves.

5. N. M. Sarna, *Genesis,* The JPS Torah Commentary (Philadelphia: Jewish Publication Society, 1989), 119.

6. Genesis 15:2.

7. Genesis 17:19.

honor and posterity. Her actions, at least at this stage, may not necessarily portray a lack of faith, but merely be a pragmatic assessment of reality.

Nevertheless, Sarai's proposal is not entirely selfless. "It may be that I shall obtain children by her." The English translation captures the note of self-interest, but misses the linguistic double entendre. Her wish is to be "built up" by this son. The Hebrew word signifies both obtaining a son (*ben*) and being built up (*b-n-h*).[8] It is the perfect expression of the role of childbearing in the Semitic worldview. The son is the heir, building up the family and sustaining its fortunes and reputation. The son to come from Hagar's womb will prosper Sarai by building up her family.

Hagar is, after all, only a slave girl.

---

8. Sarna, 119.

3

Wedding Day

So, after Abram had lived ten years in the land of Canaan, Sarai, Abram's wife, took Hagar the Egyptian, her servant, and gave her to Abram her husband as a wife. And he went in to Hagar. (Genesis 16:3–4a)

Mistress had some girls come in after breakfast.

They started with my hands. They had ways to get rid of the rough patches – and all those callouses. They did the same thing to my feet – nails, toes, heels. Then they went to work on the rest of my body – my whole body.

Even after being here this long, I don't always understand everything that's being said. The girls chattered under their breath, giggled a little, and then laughed out loud. I'm used to that – but I'm not used to being the center of attention.

All this feels strangely like wedding preparations – almost as if they're getting _me_ ready for _my_ wedding. But of course that can't possibly be – could it?!

We did all this stuff back in Egypt. All us girls would join in the work in the morning and then put on our best dresses for the evening party. The young men would lift the bride and groom up on their shoulders and we followed them through the village till we got to the groom's house. They went in. We waited outside till they finished.

Now, new clothes . . . perfume . . . a fancy hair-do . . . They lead me to Master's tent. The faint light of a lantern casts shadows all around.
I'm alone.
Then Master enters.
Now I get it. This is my wedding day.
Soon his body will lay over mine. I'm not sure what to do.
And who is waiting outside till we finish?
Just Sarai. No one else.

It is literature. This story of the Bible invites us to ask questions, and then questions our answers. It invites us in to see ourselves in its characters, to live their responses.

Hagar's life is at a turning point. As a young Egyptian slave girl she has no possibilities for bettering her situation. Perhaps she gives little thought to such things. Perhaps the reality of servitude has darkened her horizons such that her daily thought patterns are nothing more than quiet surrender to her tasks. The best she can hope for is a seat by the fire in the cool of the evening, listening to conversations in a language that's not her own, in the midst of a people she still finds strange even after more than ten years.

And yet, we don't know. There is the possibility that Hagar cherished ambitions, longings, hopes. There may yet be dreams seeking to push through the dark layers of her reality as a lily pushes through the soil. At minimum, she had known the love of a family. She had memories of a mother and probably siblings, cousins, uncles and aunts and the comfort of family visits. It was ten years or more in her past. Ten years … long enough to have grown numb from the new reality and yet not so long that the memories are completely buried.

The Middle East remains a poignant irony in matters of gender and sexuality. Though the topic is rigidly legislated by religious and social mores, it would be a mistake to think of sexuality as taboo. After all, this is the culture that produced the Song of Songs, belly dancing and Cleopatra. Female allure is as prized here as in any other culture.

In some Middle Eastern settings today, the bride and groom are celebrated with a lavish party, dancing and copious food until late into the night. Then the guests and family follow the procession to the home of the groom where the marriage is consummated – this is known as the *dakhla,* literally "the entrance." The extended family waits outside and continues its celebration after the big event.

We may surmise that Hagar had attended such ceremonies. She knew the order of events and she knew her role.

While it is impossible to peer into the young woman's mind, it is not unreasonable to consider her emotional response to the prospect of marriage to Abram. First, and most obvious, Hagar will be a second wife. The phenomenon is common throughout the Old Testament period and indeed in the contemporary Middle East. Polygamy was often a source of familial conflict and the present narrative will bear out this element.

Second, Abram could be Hagar's senior by as much as sixty years. He is eighty-seven when Hagar gives birth. Although we have no indication of her age, we know that she is of age to bear children. In the ancient world, as in much of today's Middle East, it was common to bear children well before the age of twenty. We also know that Abram and Sarai have now settled in Canaan for a period of ten years. One might reasonably suggest that Hagar was obtained in her teens (she may have been younger) and that she is now in her twenties.

It is commonly held that Hagar was granted honor by becoming the wife of Abram and that is true. However, lingering over this text may lead us to surmise that the honor came later – through the birth of a son and the possibility that Hagar would provide the sole heir to her master. The thought of being betrothed to a man sixty years older may well have held an element of dread and regret for Hagar. She is owned – an object. Her time, her energy, her body, now including her womb, are not her own. She is not granted the pleasure of sexual or social intimacy with one of the young Egyptian boys with whom she played in her youth. She was likely never celebrated as a bride. She was the implement of Abram's sired son. Just as her strong back was needed to lift firewood and cuts of meat, so her womb was needed to carry Abram's heir.

She receives his aging body into hers. Was there tenderness in Abram's caress? Did the newlyweds enjoy their union? Was there pleasant conversation in the darkness of that desert tent?

Of course, the narrator omits those details about which our curious minds may wonder. Nevertheless, the narrative suggests an arrangement which is implemented as a last resort, hardly a desirable end. The lack of any hint of emotional attraction is not without significance.

Another Old Testament marriage story stands in stark contrast, even though it, too, provides minimal detail: "Then Isaac brought her into the tent of Sarah his mother and took Rebekah, and she became his wife, and he loved her. So Isaac was comforted after his mother's death."[1] But Hagar's marriage to Abram has no observable note of joy, friendship or celebration. There is no hint that Hagar can now become a companion of the aged patriarch. It is a utilitarian arrangement, a face-saving mechanism in a culture that deals in shame and honor. The broker is the first wife, Sarai. She gives Hagar to her husband Abram as a wife, and he "goes in to" Sarai's slave girl.

We might pause here, imagining that we do not know the subsequent unfolding story. The promise to Abram was that he would have a son who would be his heir. His offspring would be as numerous as the stars in the sky. Through Abram, blessing would come to all the nations of the earth. The land of Abram's sojourning would be the possession of his seed. At this moment in the story, the seed is carried in the womb of Hagar the Egyptian.

---

1. Genesis 24:67.

The listener is invited to consider, could this utilitarian, face-saving act be the means God uses to bring about his promise? Will Hagar's child be the promised seed? Until now, we know of no reason why this will not be the case.

Subsequently, Abram, who is now Abraham, is told that his aged wife Sarah "shall become nations." The prospect is so ludicrous that Abraham laughs, and then pleads with the Lord, "Oh, that Ishmael might live before you!"[2]

It appears that for the first dozen or so years of his life, this young lad was viewed as the "son of promise." The rapid turns of events in the story deprive us of the reality of those years when Abram bonded with his son Ishmael, looking upon him as the promised son. The solution appealed to Abram such that he began to see Ishmael as the fulfillment of his dreams.

These were the years of Hagar's honor, as the mother of the heir. But we are getting ahead of the story.

---

2. Genesis 17:16, 18.

4

Rivals

*And when she saw that she had conceived, she looked
with contempt on her mistress. And Sarai said to
Abram, "May the wrong done to me be on you! I gave
my servant to your embrace, and when she saw that she
had conceived, she looked on me with contempt. May
the LORD judge between you and me!" But Abram
said to Sarai, "Behold, your servant is in your power;
do to her as you please." Then Sarai dealt harshly
with her, and she fled from her. (Genesis 16:4b–6)*

The next day, nothing had changed. I went right back to my daily chores. Yet deep down, I knew something had changed – or at least, could change.

Then came those first tell-tale signs in my body – and I knew that a baby was growing inside me. Hope was born in me, and joy grew in me, as I realized what this could mean. I began to believe that fate had finally smiled on me. Now at last I would be somebody who mattered, not just "that Egyptian girl."

The day came when I was allowed to sit and rest during the workday. I thought I deserved it. After all, I was now offering Master something that Sarai had not, and could not – and there was nothing she could do to stop it.

It served her right – but I would regret it soon enough. I guess my look of delight gave too much away.

Hagar is now Abram's wife, though presumably she continues to be viewed as the servant of Sarai, she was not merely a concubine. We may surmise that she experienced an elevation in her social standing. Now more than a slave girl, she proudly wore the badge of "wife" to her master – whose renown in the area has already been established by his prosperity and honor.

Moreover, Hagar's pregnancy would have been a boon to her sense of worth in Abram's household. She would be the mother of Abram's sole heir. In such a situation, it is hardly surprising that rivalry would develop between the two women.

The translation "looked with contempt on her mistress" is somewhat misleading. It suggests that Hagar's attitude was arrogant and hostile towards her mistress. A more literal translation would render it: "Sarai became little in Hagar's eyes." Perhaps Hagar's mistake was not explicit animosity, but maternal pride. She enjoyed her new status as it gave her an advantage over her mistress, one she had never before enjoyed.[1]

Sarai's frustration spills over in her marriage. In a scene that recalls Adam's casting blame on Eve in the garden of Eden, Sarai declares, "may the wrong done to me be on you!" After over sixty years of infertility, Sarai is clearly at her wit's end. We can imagine that the immediate conception by her slave girl has brought her simmering frustration to a boil. Her oath-like declaration is not unlike others heard in Semitic languages even today. She states that her *hamas* – violence or wrong – should come upon Abram. The word is often used of malicious lies or the experience of betrayal.[2] Sarai feels that she has been treated unfairly. She is the object of oppression. In her rage, she declares that her mistreatment should fall on someone else. The nearest object of her embittered oath is Abram himself. "May the wrong done to me be on you!"

Sarai tells him the source of her irritation. She gave her servant into Abram's embrace, or more literally, "into your lap." When Hagar conceived, Sarai grew small in her eyes. Sarai uses the same expression the narrator has employed of Hagar. Throughout the entire exchange, Sarai never mentions Hagar by name. She remains nothing more than her servant.

Sarai concludes that she has done good, but has been rewarded with evil. Once again, there is no indication in the text that Sarai is attempting to shortcut God's will by betrothing Hagar to her husband. Her perception is that she has done what is right by Abram. Her complaint points to the unfairness of

---

1. Maalouf, *Arabs in the Shadow of Israel*, 57.

2. K. A. Matthews, *Genesis 11:27–20:26*, NAC 1B, Logos Edition (Nashville: Broadman & Holman, 2005), 186.

this unfolding of events. Hagar, because she now carries Abram's child, has communicated a sense of superiority which Sarai finds unbearable. She calls on Yahweh to judge between her and her husband. The invocation of the judgment of God establishes that Sarai believes that she has done no wrong and that she suffers unjustly.

It is difficult to align fully with Sarai's complaint if one reads this narrative objectively. We can empathize with a woman whose ongoing struggle with infertility has led to an unfortunate conclusion. However, Hagar's elevation results naturally from her pregnancy and her new status as Abram's wife. Her alleged air of superiority may owe more to Sarai's sense of inferiority than to any explicit action on the part of Hagar. This is the inevitable rivalry between two wives of one man. The first has been his faithful companion through the long journey of life, but has no child. The second is a domestic slave, but she now carries his heir in her womb.

We feel the tension rise as Abram turns to his wife in desperation, giving her leave to do with her servant as she deems best. "Behold, your servant is in your power; do to her as you please." A literal translation would render it, "behold, your servant is in your hand. Do to her [what is] good in your eyes." The detail is significant, for Hagar will subsequently be directed to return and submit *under the hand* of Sarai.[3] The reference to the eyes may also be noteworthy as Sarai has become small in Hagar's eyes. This situation can now be made right. Sarai is empowered to reverse her sense of victimization.

Hagar's fate turns on the whim of the family she serves. Though she has become a wife, Abram is prepared to consign her to Sarai's authority.

"Then Sarai dealt harshly with her." Once again the translation is not entirely satisfying. "Dealing harshly" translates a widely used word that conveys subjugation and oppression, leading to despair. A better translation may be "afflict." The Hebrew word suggests "bringing someone under control and dominion by means of 'harsh treatment' that may involve physical abuse. According to Jewish interpreters, the verb implies physical and psychological abuse by Sarah aimed at subjecting Hagar."[4]

The same verb is also used of the Egyptians' oppression of the Israelites prior to the exodus.[5] Hagar the Egyptian, while living in Abram's house, suffers the same affliction that Yahweh told Abram his descendants would endure

---

3. Genesis 16:9.

4. Maalouf, *Arabs in the Shadow of Israel*, 59.

5. Exodus 1:11–12.

during their sojourn in Egypt.[6] The exodus is the story of Israel's flight from the oppression of Egypt under the providential care of Yahweh.

Hagar the Egyptian also flees from her affliction. In the words of one scholar, "Sarai does to a child of Egypt … what the Egyptians later would do to Sarai's children."[7] Will the same God who encamped around the Israelites with a pillar of cloud by day and of fire by night also care for the Egyptian slave girl whose flight will carry her in the opposite direction?

6. Genesis 15:13.

7. M. Tsevat, "Hagar and the Birth of Ishmael" in *The Meaning of the Book of Job and Other Biblical Studies: Essays on the Religion and Literature of the Hebrew Bible* (New York: Ktav, 1980), 69–70.

5

Finding Hagar

*The angel of the LORD found her by a
spring of water in the wilderness, the spring
on the way to Shur. (Genesis 16:7)*

It was so long ago – and I wasn't paying attention to the road
back then.
Is this the way we came?
Should I ask those men?
Right! So a young woman, all alone out here with a swollen belly,
who doesn't know where she's going, asks directions to Egypt. Add
to the mix that the swollen eyes and bare feet. I'm sure they'll have
lots of fun with that.

Just keep your head down – and covered. Don't make eye contact.
Just walk . . .

How stupid can I be! If anything good happens, which is almost
never, I screw it up. Why couldn't I just toe the line, suck it up
as I'd done for years? I had to go and flaunt my good fortune in
Sarai's face.

Now look at me. I'm somewhere between a home that has forgotten
me and another one where I'm just the slave girl without a name. I
can't get back to the first one and God knows there's no going back
to Sarai.

Dying would be God's mercy right now.
Water! Where can I find water?
Wait, just there – is that a spring? At last I'll cool my parched
throat!
Wait . . . I hear steps behind me. Just keep walking. Head down and
keep walking. Keep breathing.
I swear, someone's running after me.
God, help me!

Shur is located in the northwest Sinai, a desert region that must be crossed when traveling from Canaan to Egypt. Hagar is making her way back to Egypt when she is "found" by the angel of Yahweh. In the Bible, when God "finds" someone, it usually implies he has chosen them for a special role and calling. God "found" his people in the desert;[1] he "found" his servant David;[2] now, he finds Hagar.[3]

Who is "the angel of the LORD"?

I honed my mental image of angels lying awake in my grandmother's guestroom. The image on the bedroom wall showed a young boy and girl in tattered clothes making their way across a rickety bridge in the dark of night. Unknown to them, the pair was overshadowed by a majestic female angel with gigantic outstretched wings, her arms enfolding the wayward children, ensuring their safe passage. I supposed she was their guardian angel, carrying out her mission to protect and bless those under her care.

Hagar's encounter, to the casual observer, is reminiscent of that scene. A poor lost girl needs to be "touched by an angel" – and an angel shows up just as despair was certain to overtake our young heroine.

However, this story is saying something more. The Hebrews were not privy to centuries of European Renaissance art with its portrayal of glowing halos and feathered wings. This angel is infinitely more interesting. This angel is simply *malak Yawheh* – the sent one of Yahweh or simply, Yahweh's messenger.

Since context is our best clue to discerning the meaning of a passage, we begin by asking what identity the narrator ascribes to this messenger.

Although it means getting ahead of our story, we note that this angel speaks on his own authority: "I will surely multiply your offspring."[4] The messenger then proceeds to lay out the destiny of the child in Hagar's womb. The text solves the riddle by stating that Hagar named the being who spoke with her. Literally it reads: "So she called the name of Yahweh, the one speaking to her …" (In reading the Old Testament, it helps to recall that LORD – when in all capital letters – denotes YHWH or Yahweh, the Hebrew personal name of God.)

According to the narrator, this messenger does not merely carry the authority of Yahweh as a delegate or an emissary. This *is* Yahweh – the unfathomable God of the Hebrews, the one eternal God whom no eye has

---

1. Deuteronomy 32:10.
2. Psalm 89:20.
3. Maalouf, *Arabs in the Shadow of Israel*, 62.
4. Genesis 16:10.

seen nor mind conceived. Yet he comes. He comes seeking and finding the Egyptian slave girl of Sarai. Yahweh pursues Hagar and finds her.

The Hebrew prophets, who vigorously upheld the oneness of God, did not begin at the conceptual level as did the Greeks. Their starting point was neither an "unmoved mover" nor a "non-contingent essence," but a person with whom they walked and talked and wrestled.

Abraham met with Yahweh more than once. He had Sarah cook for Yahweh and offered him a meal. He stood at the ready as a servant while Yahweh enjoyed his hospitality. Perhaps this is what Jesus was referring to when he said, "Your father Abraham rejoiced that he would see my day. He saw it and was glad."[5] It was also *malak Yahweh* who called to Abraham from heaven to halt the sacrifice of Isaac.

Jacob encountered Yahweh twice – first at Bethel, and later in the dark night of Peniel.[6] In the latter encounter, he clung to the mysterious assailant, refusing to let him go until he received his blessing. Jacob declared that he had seen God face to face and yet lived. Much later, Hosea refers to Jacob's encounter with the *malak* and proceeds to interpret this as his meeting God himself.[7]

Moses spoke with Yahweh "face to face, as a man speaks to his friend."[8] What's more, Yahweh sent his "angel" (*malak*) before the Israelites, warning them that he would by no means pardon their iniquity because his name was in him. The implication is that the angel has the power to forgive sin.[9]

The same angel appears to Gideon, commanding him to "go in this might of yours and save Israel from the hand of Midian."[10]

These appearances of the angel of the Lord command our attention. At times, the angel is identified as Yahweh himself. At other times, there seems to be some distinction. This dynamic of a shared yet distinct identity led the church fathers, as well as more recent interpreters, to view the angel as a preincarnate appearance of the divine Logos, the eternal Son.

No doubt some will say we are reading the theology of the church councils back into the Old Testament text. But before the church councils spoke of the one God in three persons, no less a person than Jesus marveled at the unbelief

---

5. John 8:56.

6. Genesis 28:10–17; 32:22–32.

7. Hosea 12:4.

8. Exodus 33:1.

9. Matthews, *Genesis*, 189.

10. Judges 6:14.

of his contemporaries, warning them that by not believing him, they were rejecting Moses who wrote about him. Apparently, Jesus did not consider it strange that he was found in the Jewish scriptures.

The eternal Son, eternally beloved, "did not regard equality with God a thing to be grasped, but emptied himself, by taking the form of a servant."[11] Paul describes Jesus in this way. The discovery that he was doing a very similar thing even *before* the incarnation serves only to deepen our sense of awe and majesty as we contemplate the divine love.

Those familiar with the story of Jesus will not be surprised that he would find a woman by a water source. Have you ever considered that Hagar was pursued by the same person who spoke with the woman at the well? That the one who called Zacchaeus down from the sycamore tree now calls Sarai's slave girl? Could it be that the person who sent the Gadarene home now sends the Egyptian back to her mistress? This reality casts quite a different light on the Hagar story. It is only in this light that we can fully appreciate Hagar and her son.

For Hagar, there is no mistaking this person. She knows whom she has seen. This is Yahweh – the same God who promised Abram that his descendants would be as many as the stars of heaven. Now he has come to her. Hagar was lost. Now, she is found.

---

11. Philippians 2:6b–7a.

6

Questions

And he said, "Hagar, servant of Sarai, where have you come from and where are you going?" She said, "I am fleeing from my mistress Sarai." The angel of the LORD said to her, "Return to your mistress and submit to her." (Genesis 16:8–9)

How did he know my name?
And how did he know Sarai's name and that I am her servant?
He must have followed me all the way from Bethel. But I don't
recognize him.

He not only knows my name, but he spoke it. He called me by my
name! – not just "Sarai's girl" like everybody else. I thought my
name was forgotten, buried back in Egypt.

"Where have you come from?"
I can't answer that question. Maybe I know where I've come from –
sort of – but the way I got there in the first place was totally out of
my control. Is that what he means? Does he mean "<u>Where</u> have you
come from?" Or does he mean "What brought you here?"

"Where are you going?"
There is no answer. I have nowhere to go. If he insists, I'll just say
I'm going to Egypt. The strange thing, though, is that he even
asked me a question. No one wants to hear what I think, but this
man's paying attention. He tracked me here, and now he's waiting
for my answer. Can I risk it?

I'll just say what he already knows – it's all I really know anyway.
What's the worst he could do? Make me go back?
"I am fleeing from my mistress Sarai."

Hagar is lost, geographically, in the wilderness between Egypt and Canaan. She is also lost existentially. She was taken away from her family and culture, probably at quite a young age. For at least ten years, perhaps more, Hagar has been a servant. Her self-determination and initiative have been subservient to the whims of her mistress. Hagar has not made her own decisions or set her own trajectory. She finds herself pregnant and abused, hopelessly confused and unsure what her future will be, or even if there will be a future.

We should not too quickly pass over the two questions posed by the angel of Yahweh. To begin with, his calling Hagar by her personal name is striking. No one else in the story has done so. We only know Hagar's name because the narrator felt it important to tell us. The angel calls her by name and then, as if to assure her that he is aware of her circumstances, also pronounces her role: "Hagar, servant of Sarai …"

Perhaps the angel is revealing just enough for Hagar to recognize that this is no ordinary encounter. He knows her affliction at the hand of Sarai, but he also acknowledges that she is more than a mere servant girl. She is Hagar. She has a name – and an identity which preceded her servitude.

As suggested before, after his incarnation, the angel of Yahweh interacts similarly with another woman by a water source. He knows her marital history and her sordid past, and mentions enough of it to let her know that she is not dealing with a normal traveler passing through the village. This man is homing in on precisely what is tormenting her soul, though she is too terrified to speak about it openly. She must have realized that she could not hide from this man. We may surmise that her response vacillated between terror and shame on the one hand and a dim hope that someone understood on the other.

No doubt Hagar, too, was taken aback by the angel's greeting. If he knows her to be Sarai's slave girl, he also knows that she is running away. A runaway slave is stolen property. Will he keep her secret? Or will he denounce her, adding to her shame and despair?

Neither. Rather, he commands that she return. This is no promise that everything will be fine once she obeys. The command is to return and "submit to her." The latter verb, in the original Hebrew, is a three-word phrase, literally "submit under her hand." The phrase "under her hand" recalls verse 6, where Abram tells Sarai that her servant is "in your power" (literally, "behold your servant is in your hand"). The word "submit" is a derivative form of the same verb used in verse 6: "Sarai dealt harshly with her." The narrator is giving the reader a clear signal that all will not be rosy when Hagar returns. She is commanded by the angel to return to the harsh treatment from which she has fled.

If we were to stop here, we would have to conclude that the angel has brought bad news to Hagar. There is no escape for her, no salvation. She is doomed to a life of affliction and subservience. Fortunately, the story does not stop here; the angel has much more to say to the Egyptian slave girl.

But we should pause and contemplate this angel – the messenger of Yahweh, whom we have come to believe is the preincarnate eternal Son of God.

We have likened his encounter with Hagar to a New Testament encounter with the Samaritan woman by the well. In that meeting, Jesus surprises his followers, reversing the cultural norms of his day by conversing openly and freely with a woman. He renders himself ceremonially unclean according to Jewish custom by drinking from the woman's vessel, sleeping two nights in the Samaritan village and eating their food. By breaking with tradition, Jesus demonstrates his passion to seek and save those who are lost. It goes beyond a mere mandate handed down to him, for he declares, "my food is to do the will of him who sent me."[1] The implication is that Jesus thoroughly enjoyed his encounter with the Samaritan woman and found it so satisfying that he was willing to forego eating.

But Jesus also had some seemingly harsh and confrontational words for the woman. She was told to bring her husband, though Jesus made it clear that the man was not her husband but only her consort, and that she had five husbands previous to him. Her question concerning the proper place of worship received the stunning response that soon neither Jerusalem nor Gerizim would be the proper place of worship since worship would no longer be determined by geography. No doubt this uncharacteristic response shakes her world, but it also opens up to her the possibility of her inclusion among these worshipers who worship "in spirit and truth." Then Jesus adds a seemingly harsh corrective: "you worship what you do not know; we worship what we know, for salvation is from the Jews."[2]

Jesus, in his earthly ministry, went to great lengths to get to know and converse with those who fell beyond the pale of proper Judaism. He intentionally sought out outsiders and brought them in. Yet, he did not gush over them. His was no naive credulity that loses orientation and rootedness. Jesus encountered outsiders with care and compassion, but also with correctives.

Hagar's flight was madness. God's will for Hagar was that she should submit herself under the harsh hand of Sarai. She must return there. It was only there that she would discover the blessing that the angel would soon reveal to her.

---

1. John 4:34.
2. John 4:22.

Jesus had no qualms about asking each of his disciples to take up their cross and follow him. He made it clear to James and John that they would need to drink the cup which he himself would drink. His call to a rich young man was to sell all he had, distribute his goods to the poor and then come and follow him. Many other examples could be cited; the point being that Jesus never apologized, equivocated or mitigated his call to suffering.

We should see the command to return to Sarai as a test of Hagar's discipleship. Will she believe the promises of the angel to the point of following his directive even though it will mean certain suffering for her?

"In the world you will have tribulation. But take heart; I have overcome the world."[3]

---

3. John 16:33b.

7

The Promise

The angel of the LORD also said to her, "I will surely multiply your offspring so that they cannot be numbered for multitude." And the angel of the LORD said to her,

"Behold, you are pregnant
and shall bear a son.
You shall call his name Ishmael,

because the LORD has listened to your affliction." (Genesis 16:10–11)

At last, at last, I know where I'm going.

I can't stop thinking about what he said – and rolling it around in my heart.

I've heard it before. It sounds so much like what Master used to say – that Yahweh was going to multiply his offspring, that his offspring would be like the stars of heaven.

If it were anybody else, and if he didn't sound so sure of what he was saying, we would have just laughed. But it's hard to laugh at a man like Abram. I was supposed to give him an heir. That was my role. His stubborn confidence created all this mess.

He said God promised him. And now, I heard it too. He said he would multiply my offspring "so that they cannot be numbered for multitude." Hagar's offspring a multitude?! I can hear the laughter already. I'd better just keep my mouth shut.

But I know where I'm going. I'm headed back to Sarai – for better or for worse. But I'm having a son – and his name is my hope. God heard when she treated me harshly. He heard! I never dreamed anyone would hear me, least of all that HE would hear me. Somehow, that changes everything.

Ishmael . . .

The angel's tone pivots starkly. He began by sending Hagar back to live in subjugation under the hand of Sarai, whose harsh treatment had left her no choice but to run away. The promise that follows, though, is of such magnitude that we risk skimming over it without grasping its glorious implications.

The language is familiar. We recognize it, as would the ancient Hebrews, as being the language of covenant. God had promised the patriarchs – Abraham, Isaac and Jacob – that their progeny would multiply, spreading from east to west and north to south. The promises were so all-encompassing that they seemed to be exaggerations, expressions of wishful thinking with no grounding in reality. Yet, there they are, in the ancient scriptures of the Jews – promises that the heirs of these patriarchs would fill the earth and become as numerous as the sand on the shore or the stars of heaven.

It is not difficult to believe that Hagar knew the details of Abram's own encounters with Yahweh and the amazing promises of a multitude of offspring dwelling securely in the land given by this same God.

Can we not also imagine that Hagar would have found some way to tell Abram that she herself had heard a promise from a strange visitor she met in the wilderness of Shur? Perhaps, after Hagar's return, Abram became even more convinced that the young son in her womb was the fulfillment of the promise.

Surely the angel's words to Hagar suggested to Abram that Hagar's son was indeed the long-awaited son. Yet Yahweh would visit Abram again, and this time stipulate that the fulfillment of his promise would come through Sarai, now renamed Sarah. Indeed, kings and nations would come from her.

Our knowledge of subsequent biblical history should not detract from what is taking place in this scene with Hagar. Hagar's son is not the son of Abram's promise. He is, however, the son of *Hagar's* promise – and that is equally stunning. The slave girl, the Egyptian immigrant, the oppressed surrogate wife receives a promise that is reflective of God's covenant promises to the patriarchs – *her* offspring will be multiplied beyond number.

Why Hagar? The slave girl appears to be plucked from the pages of history and plopped into this story. She is a passive character in the narrative. Until this point, the only words we hear from her lips is that she is fleeing from her mistress Sarai. Yet, with the exception of Mary the mother of Jesus, she is the only woman in all of Scripture to receive such a sweeping promise, and the first since Eve to encounter Yahweh. What is the story telling us through this woman?

Just as the amazing promise made to Hagar reflects God's promise to the patriarchs, so his naming of Ishmael is a precursor, a pointer, to what will transpire among the twelve tribes of Jacob.

Abram had granted Sarai license to do with her servant as she pleased, and the result was Hagar's subjugation and abuse. The slave girl had no advocate, no recourse and no rights. She had no alternative but to flee. No one heeded her. No one cared that she bore the brunt of Sarai's frustrated maternal longing.

Yishma' el – Ishmael: "God hears."

We are not far into the story of Genesis. Only a few chapters previously, Adam and Eve made the fateful decision to trust the words of the serpent. The tragic result had brought violence into the first family as Cain slayed his brother Abel in a fit of jealousy aroused by an act of worship. The slain brother's blood cried to God from the ground. Later, we observe the downward spiral of mankind's alienation from God. As sexual exploitation and violence reach a crescendo, "The LORD saw that the wickedness of man was great in the earth, and that every intention of the thoughts of his heart was only evil continually."[1] In response to this downward spiral of alienation, God intervenes through Noah, judging yet renewing the earth through the flood. After Babel, mankind's failed attempt to establish autonomy from God, Noah's descendants are scattered and fill the earth with diverse peoples, nations and languages.

We reach a watershed in the narrative with God's call of Abram in Genesis 12. A means of bringing blessing to the nations of the world is identified. The blessing will come through Abram who will be made a great nation. Very soon, however, Abram's progeny will find themselves under the hand of a cruel taskmaster in Egypt. But God hears their outcry. At long last, God hears.

The story of Hagar serves as a precursor of what will transpire in the future. The Egyptian is oppressed in the house of Abram. Soon the house of Abraham will be oppressed in the land of Egypt. Yahweh hears the affliction of the slave girl just as he has "seen the affliction of my people who are in Egypt and have heard their cry because of their taskmasters. I know their sufferings."[2] He brings them out of Egypt in a dramatic act of salvation.

Hagar's experience reflects that of the children of Israel. Her exile is in reverse order to theirs. She is taken from Egypt into the land of Canaan. She is subjected to servitude and, when that servitude becomes harsh and unbearable, she escapes. Hagar's promised land is not a "land flowing with milk and honey" but a return to her mistress. She is to abide in Abram's house.

We may go further still in our analogy. The tribes of Jacob return to the land, their heritage, with experiential awareness that God has heard their

---

1. Genesis 6:5.
2. Exodus 3:7.

cry. They are reconstituted as a people and the fear of them falls on the surrounding nations.

Hagar returns to Sarai, as a servant, but with head held high. Something has transpired. The rivalry that characterized the relationship is now eased. Hagar's affliction was seen. Her cry was heard. Hers is the honor of carrying the son of her master, Abram, but she need no longer flaunt her privilege. The angel of Yahweh encountered her with a destiny of promise and hope. Paul's maxim from another era – "The old has passed away; behold, the new has come"[3] – applies to Hagar, for she has encountered Christ and trusted his word.

The long delay of thirteen years before Sarah will give birth to Isaac demonstrates the miraculous nature of the conception. It may also serve another purpose: to allow the young Ishmael sufficient time to mature and enjoy his father's affection before being cast out with his mother yet again.

In ancient times, the God of Abraham heard the desperate cries of a slave girl and intervened to secure for her a future and a hope. He is the same yesterday, today and forever. Another highly favored woman declared "he has looked on the humble estate of his servant. For behold, from now on all generations will call me blessed; … he has brought down the mighty from their thrones and exalted those of humble estate."[4]

Hagar, the Egyptian slave girl, a multitude? Who would have dreamed?

---

3. 2 Corinthians 5:17.
4. Luke 1:48, 52.

8

Donkey Man

"He shall be a wild donkey of a man,
his hand against everyone
and everyone's hand against him,
and he shall dwell over against all his
kinsmen." (Genesis 16:12)

Just as he said "wild donkey," I noticed a few, just beyond the spring at Shur, over on the rise. I caught sight of them just over his shoulder. Maybe he knew. I saw quite a few on the way here, too – always up on the heights, away from where people walk.

What did he mean, though?
"His hand against everyone and everyone's hand against him."
Ha! Sounds like my boy might have a stubborn streak – and he's sure going to need it. At least he won't be under somebody's hand like I am. Maybe he'll help me find my freedom, too. And he has a place to live, a place all his own. It sounds like he'll be near his kin, yet separate too. I'm glad he won't be cut off from family like I was. But – who's his kin?

So much to think about . . .

This verse has been tragically misunderstood. Read through our contemporary lens, the verse indicates that Ishmael will, frankly, be a jackass. He will have the traits of a donkey – stubborn obstinacy on the one hand and stupidity on the other. It's not a pretty picture.

Is this just another of the Bible's indiscretions such as the "cursed Moabites," the "Cretan liars" or the "Canaanite dogs"? The descriptor embarrasses us postmoderns. Should we not be more tolerant? Is the Bible sanctioning racism? Is God warning us not to expect anything good from the likes of Ishmael? Will Ishmael be a cause of perennial enmity and ignorance among the peoples of the Middle East?

For most contemporary readers, this is the implicit understanding of the text, even if we are reluctant to put it in such candid terms. The declaration of the angel appears to be a curse, consigning Ishmael to a destiny of violence and stubborn resistance to authority.

What are we to make of it?

When reading the Bible, we venture into a library of some of the most ancient literary works in the world. We are separated from the authors by millennia and vast cultural chasms. Inevitably, we read the text as modern people, with our own background – culture, education, social identity, etc. – dictating our understanding, often unaware of how our context shapes our view. Does this mean that a true understanding is beyond our grasp? Do we give up? No, but we should be cautious in our interpretation. Reading the Bible with humility means we must sometimes reserve judgment and seek assistance from those who specialize in understanding its message.

Two major considerations may cause us to reconsider previously held views of the so-called "curse of Ishmael." The first consideration is context. If our surface reading of a text appears inconsistent with the surrounding sentences and paragraphs, this is a clue that we need to seek an alternative understanding.

In the context of Hagar's dialogue with the angel of Yahweh, we noticed that the angel "found" Hagar – a phrase often used in the Old Testament for God saving an individual or a people. He calls Hagar by name and addresses questions to her. Finally, he directs Hagar to return and submit "under the hand" of Sarai. This must have been a hard word for Hagar to hear. However, the very next sentence conveys stunning good news. Hagar's offspring will become a multitude. This is recognizable as covenantal language used elsewhere in Genesis when Yahweh reveals his intentions to Abraham, Isaac and Jacob.

Next, God names the boy in Hagar's womb "Ishmael." It is a name that will be a constant reminder of God's loving care of Hagar even during her subjugation and enslavement. This, too, can only be understood as a positive promise of God's attentiveness to Hagar even in her dark moments.

Then comes verse 12, with the two problematic images – Ishmael as a "wild donkey of a man" and "his hand against everyone and everyone's hand against him."

Following this verse, we find Hagar naming the God who spoke with her. We will look at this in greater detail in a subsequent chapter; suffice to say that Hagar's naming of God is her recognition of and gratitude for his gracious intervention in her life.

So verse 12, which appears on the surface to be quite negative, falls among some very positive elements in the dialogue – the covenantal promise, the naming of Ishmael and Hagar's naming of God. If verse 12 is understood as a curse, it means that the tone of the dialogue takes a dramatic and unanticipated shift, with the angel pulling Hagar in two opposing directions – blessing and cursing.

The second major consideration is the meaning of the words as they are used in their original language. Generally, our translations of the Bible serve us very well, but there are occasions when knowledge of the original language can clarify the author's intention. This is one such instance.

The "donkey" spoken of here is not the normal domesticated beast of burden which we imagine. The word is *pere* – a wild donkey that roams the rugged deserts of the Middle East even today. This is the animal that God mentions when he asks Job and his friends: "Who has let the wild donkey [*pere*] go free? Who has loosed the bonds of the swift donkey?";[1] Jeremiah describes a famine so intense that even the wild donkeys suffer: "The wild donkeys stand on the bare heights; they pant for air like jackals; their eyes fail because there is no vegetation";[2] and Isaiah 32:14 describes a deserted city as inhabited by wild donkeys.

I first encountered the "desert donkey" when I was taking a class on pre-Islamic poetry – the ancient Arabs composed eloquent verse describing their desert environment. The desert donkey of the Arabs was not the stupid and insolent beast of burden, derogatively known as a jackass. Rather, this animal combines at least four noteworthy characteristics: (1) a strong will; (2) a desert

---

1. Job 39:5.
2. Jeremiah 14:6.

habitation; (3) a free-moving, nomadic life; and (4) it scorns civilization and domestication.[3]

The description is apt for Bedouin and nomadic people such as Ishmael's descendants.

Given that the entire passage, with the exception of the command to return to Sarai, has comforted Hagar, it is likely that this animal is not a symbol of obstinate stupidity, but of independence and the determined refusal to bow to domestic servitude. The desert donkey may well have been recognized by Hagar as a symbol of freedom and self-determination. And so, her son's being likened to a "wild donkey" is understood by her to be a reversal of her condition. Her son, unlike herself, will throw off the fetters of servitude. He will roam free and determine his own destiny. Indeed, one Jewish interpreter understands the passage in precisely this way:

> Like the wild ass among the beasts, so are the Ishmaelites among men. In their nature and destiny they call to mind the sturdy, fearless, and fleet-footed Syrian onager (Heb. *pere*), who inhabits the wilderness and is almost impossible to domesticate. Jeremiah describes the wild ass of the desert: "snuffing the wind in her eagerness, whose passion none can restrain." Hagar, the abused slave woman subjected to the harsh discipline of her mistress, will produce a people free and undisciplined.[4]

The second image is also elucidated by observing the original language: "his hand against everyone and everyone's hand against him." The structure is much more succinct in Hebrew – a mere five words. It follows immediately after the "wild donkey" phrase, further defining the character of Hagar's son.

Recall that the image of the hand has already appeared twice in this chapter. In verse 6, Abram reminds Sarai that her servant is "in your power," literally "in her hand" or under her authority. The same preposition is used here as in verse 12 where it is translated "against." The angel commands her to return to Sarai, submitting herself "under her hand." Thus the hand is an expression of mastery and authority, recalling Hagar's servitude.

Ishmael's hand being "against everyone" or "upon all" need not be interpreted as enmity. It may be simply a further nuance of the "wild donkey" phrase, affirming to Hagar that although she must be subject to Sarai ("in

---

3. Maalouf, *Arabs in the Shadow of Israel*, 70. Maalouf draws these four characteristics from Imad Nicola Shehadeh, "Ishmael in Relation to the Promises of Abraham" (ThM thesis, Dallas Theological Seminary, 1986), 79.

4. Sarna, *Genesis*, 121.

her hand"), her son will be subject to no man. The message would have been a great comfort to Hagar and the context indicates that she understood the description as a blessing, not a curse.

The final descriptor has also been problematic. Literally, the text says that he will live "before the face (in front) of all his brothers." Recent translations render it "over against" his brothers. This is precisely what happened. Later in Genesis we are told that Ishmael's twelve sons settled "from Havilah to Shur, which is opposite Egypt in the direction of Assyria. He settled *over against* all his kinsmen"[5] – the precise phrase which is used in Genesis 16:12 – designating the homeland of the Ishmaelites. While Hagar has fled from before "the face" of Sarah,[6] her son will live openly "in the face" (in plain view) of his brothers.[7]

For years, the popular New International Version (NIV) was the standard text of English-speaking Christians, and it remains so for many. The NIV translates the phrase as follows: "and he will live in hostility towards all his brothers." The translation skews the meaning and is uncalled for. Unfortunately, it has reaffirmed the prevailing impression that Ishmael was a man of warfare who would continually incite conflict with his brother. Such was not the case in the times of the patriarchs and it need not be the case now.

Genesis 16:12 foresees a life of protected isolation for Ishmael. He will be as free and independent as the desert donkey, living in proximity to his brother Isaac in the desert steppe of a region we know today as the Sinai Peninsula of Egypt, southern Israel, Jordan and Saudi Arabia.

The three phrases of this verse were likely understood by Hagar to be a reversal of her domestic servitude. The angel has commanded her to return to her mistress, but her son will cast off the bonds of slavery and live as a free and fiercely independent man. He will have a homeland in proximity to his brothers – a desirable situation, and one of which Hagar has been deprived. Ishmael is not cursed, but blessed.

Hagar, our humble heroine, must have believed the promise, for she acted promptly on the command, returning to her place of servitude as Sarai's slave girl.

---

5. Genesis 25:18.

6. Genesis 16:8.

7. Toba Spitzer, "'Where Do You Come from and Where Are You Going?' Hagar and Sarah Encounter God," *The Reconstructionist* (Fall, 1998): 11.

9

El Ro'i

*So she called the name of the LORD who spoke
to her, "You are a God of seeing," for she said,
"Truly here I have seen him who looks after me."
Therefore the well was called Beer-lahai-roi; it lies
between Kadesh and Bered. (Genesis 16:13–14)*

All those years in Egypt, I was always passed over. No one noticed me. No one saw me. Then I became Sarai's slave girl. And still no one saw me. The only time I was noticed was when the food was bad, burned, or late.

All my life, no one paid attention to me. I was always left sitting on the outside. They talked, I listened. They ate, I served. They married, I bathed and dressed them. They had families, I had work. Even when she gave me to Master, I just happened to be there. My job was to spread my legs and carry a baby. But I didn't matter.

It all changed today. Oh everyone else may think nothing changed, but I know that everything changed – because he saw me. He must have. When I had no clue, no hope, no future, he found me. He kept running behind me till he found me. He gave me my destiny. It's not something I would have asked for, but he knew – he knew what Hagar needed.

I'd like to show my gratitude by offering a sacrifice, but I don't have an animal. So let me do this instead before I start back – He named my boy. Now I want to give him a name.
The God who sees me.
Ah, that's perfect.
I'll never forget this day or the God who sees me.

Hagar is the first and only woman to designate a name for the God she has met and with whom she has interacted. Indeed, no other Old Testament character conferred a name on deity.[1] That's remarkable.

Jacob named a place – Peniel – marking his encounter with God; but Hagar names God himself. Hagar is a theologian (in the true sense of the word), describing the God she has encountered as one who sees personally and up close, but also as one who is seen. God saw her. She also perceived God. The unfathomable and invisible God has appeared as the "seeing one."

The narrator is unequivocal, so we should be as well. It was Yahweh who was speaking with her. This is the same Lord who inaugurated a covenant with Abram and revealed to him the future of his descendants. The Lord who changed his name to Abraham since he would be the father of a multitude of nations. The one who promised that Sarah would bear a son. The same Yahweh who, along with two other heavenly guests, appeared to Abraham by the Oaks of Mamre – chatting with the patriarch, eating his food and resting while discussing the fate of Sodom and of Abraham's nephew, Lot. One wonders if Hagar, now back in the household of Abraham, recognized the heavenly visitor. The text is silent.

It cannot be forgotten and it must not be overlooked. The God of the patriarchs – Yahweh by name – appeared to the Egyptian slave girl and gave her amazing promises, which she believed. She responded by giving Yahweh a name.

El. It is God's name, a commonly used name for the deity in the Semitic languages of the ancient Near East. The patriarchs used it when referring to God, often with a descriptor – such as *El-Elyon* (God Most High), *El-Shaddai* (God Almighty) – which expressed attributes of God they had come to know through personal experience.

Ro'i. The word can be rendered in different ways depending on how it is vocalized. The ambiguity of the Old Testament writers may be intentional, expressing an array of meanings.

"God of seeing" is a possible rendering. It implies that God sees, and therefore knows, all.

"God of *my* seeing" is another possible translation. Here, Hagar is the seeing one while God is the object of her vision. She marvels over the reality that she has seen God and interacted with him face to face.[2]

---

1. K. W. Larsen, "El Roi," *The Lexham Bible Dictionary, Logos Edition* (Bellingham, WA: Lexham Press, 2016).

2. Sarna, *Genesis*, 121.

"The God who sees me." This rendering has the greatest appeal. The terse phrase expresses the Egyptian woman's incredulity that she would be the object of God's attentiveness and care. There may also be a subtle recalling of Hagar's misstep when her mistress "became small" in her eyes.[3] For Hagar, her own smallness and insignificance are brushed aside by the reality of God's thoughtful care extended to her in the promises of the divine visitor.

The second phrase, "Truly here I have seen him who looks after me," is equally rich, though also difficult to express in a single sentence. Some translators perceive Hagar as astonished that she has survived the vision of God: "Have I even remained alive here after seeing him?" (NASB). Others have suggested, "I have seen God after he saw me" or "Would I have gone here indeed looking for him that looks after me?"[4] A literal translation could be "for she said, even this far, you have looked after me, seeing."

Perhaps the simple slave girl is amazed that God has followed her all the way to Shur, but this seems to miss the depth of emotion in her declaration. Hagar's life has been a journey of subjugation. Any ability or capability she might have developed was at the disposal of another. She was taken from her home and homeland at a young age and served the household needs of Abram's family, and particularly Abram's wife, Sarai. Her incredulity has little to do with the distance she has traveled from Canaan. It has everything to do with the journey of her life. She who has never been seen is now seen.

In a narrative where Hagar appears as a cog in the wheel of domestic servitude and exploitation, she now manifests a unique power, issuing from her encounter with the living God. She bestows a name upon divinity. It is a type of resurrection – a transfer from helplessness and passivity to initiative, action, power – resulting from the encounter with Yahweh.

I recall an occasion when one of my daughters was particularly intent on having my full attention. I was often preoccupied, but this time she would not have it. In her frustration, she put her little hands on either side of my face, using all her force to redirect my gaze toward her. Her blue eyes stared directly into mine as she pleaded "Daddy, look at me!"

The exchange remains etched on my memory as a poignant reminder that we all long to be seen, to be noticed. What is true for children is also true for grown-ups.

---

3. Matthews, *Genesis*.
4. Spitzer, "Where Do You Come From," 12.

Hagar has just peered behind the curtain and understood what had previously been unthinkable. She is seen. God pursues. God hears. God sees. More importantly and incredibly, God sees *her*.

Her return to slavery will be no small challenge. Nevertheless, her destiny is secure because of the all-seeing and wonderfully caring God.

The name that Hagar gives the angel continues to speak volumes for the one who has ears to hear. Can we not also perceive more deeply the identity of the angel in this name? Did not the latter "in flesh" appearance of this same angel express, in the most vivid way imaginable, God's attentive care to bring us back into relation with himself? Did he not call us friends and not slaves? Did he not make us his sons and daughters?

The encounter with Hagar is a vivid and beautiful precursor of Jesus's incarnation, when God "looks after us even this far" to bolster us for the difficult road ahead by securing for us a destiny that enables us to hold our heads high and trust him.

10

Oh That Ishmael Might Live!

*And Hagar bore Abram a son, and Abram called
the name of his son, whom Hagar bore, Ishmael.
Abram was eighty-six years old when Hagar
bore Ishmael to Abram. (Genesis 16:15–16)*

*Then Abraham fell on his face and laughed and said to
himself, "Shall a child be born to a man who is a hundred
years old? Shall Sarah, who is ninety years old, bear a
child?" And Abraham said to God, "Oh that Ishmael
might live before you!" God said, "No, but Sarah your wife
shall bear you a son, and you shall call his name Isaac.
I will establish my covenant with him as an everlasting
covenant for his offspring after him. As for Ishmael, I have
heard you; behold, I have blessed him and will make him
fruitful and multiply him greatly. He shall father twelve
princes, and I will make him into a great nation. But I
will establish my covenant with Isaac, whom Sarah shall
bear to you at this time next year." (Genesis 17:17–21)*

When I told him about the angel and the promises, he nodded like he understood. I knew he believed me because when the boy was born he named him exactly what the angel told me.

I've watched Abram for all these long years, and if there's one thing I know about him it's this: he's a man who believes in his God – "Seeing One." I told him what I named the well, too, and I think he approved.

Twelve years have passed since that day the angel found me. I'll never forget that first time Abram took my son – his son too – in his arms. His grin stretched from one ear to the other. God bless that man! All these years he's been waiting so patiently. I think Sarai and I could finally agree on something – that giving Abram a son was a good thing! Even though the going hasn't been easy, I'm glad I was the one to do it.

Things have settled down since the angel visited me. I did what he said – put myself under Sarai's command. But it's worked out. Maybe I'm the one who has changed the most.

Ishmael has grown. He's nearly a man now. I can't believe such a fine boy came from me – and I think Abram is just as proud of him as I am.

When a new baby comes, everything changes. If that's true in our day, we can imagine that Ishmael's arrival marked a day of celebration in Abram's household. The female rivalry would have faded into the background as the women fussed over the new boy who needed constant care and attention. We wouldn't be straying far from the tone of the narrative if we assume that Abram held Ishmael in his arms and dreamed that this little boy, with his dark and charming features, would be the fulfillment of the promise given to him by God.

That was not to be, of course. Yet, it may serve us well to pause and consider that, at this point in the story, Ishmael is the only candidate for fulfilling that promise. As far as we know, Sarai is not integral to the story. The promise was to Abraham and the fulfillment required a son. Thanks to Sarai's ingenuity, the story could now unfold. And so it did for almost fourteen years. Between the ages of eighty-six and ninety-nine, Abram was not aware that the promise would be fulfilled through another son. We can imagine that his soul became entwined with young Ishmael and that the old man loved him dearly. Perhaps that will help *us* to love him, too.

The visitation of Yahweh shed new light on Ishmael's future and was almost certainly a shock to Abram. The promise of multiplication was reiterated: "I am God Almighty [*El-Shaddai*]; walk before me, and be blameless, that I may make my covenant between me and you, and may multiply you greatly."[1] Abram fell on his face.

Then God changed his name. We know that in Hebrew thought the name reflects the character and destiny of the person. The narrative of Abraham is carried along by the naming of persons and God. Two names will be changed, and a third designated, in this encounter.

Abram means "great father." "But your name shall be Abraham, for I have made you the father of a multitude of nations."[2] Perhaps Abram thought his name was a cruel irony since, for his first fourscore years, the "great father" had no children. Only since the birth of Ishmael had his life circumstances allowed him to carry his name without shame.

The promises of Abram's God, however, seemed to flow out of some source of infinite generosity. "The stars of heaven" he had heard before. "The sand on the shore" he would hear subsequently. Now his attentive ear strained to grasp the scope of the visitor's promise: "the father of a multitude of nations" – Abraham.

---

1. Genesis 17:2.
2. Genesis 17:5.

Nor would Sarai's name remain unchanged, for she would bear Abraham a son. She would be Sarah – a princess. Indeed, she would be the matriarch of nations and kings of nations would issue from her.

Abraham was no less startled by the revelation than you or I would be. He was now one hundred years old, and Sarah was ninety. Like us, his rational mind stumbles over the implausibility of the promise, and he pleads, "Oh that Ishmael might live before you!"

The patriarch's supplication was not answered as he anticipated, for Isaac would be the heir and fulfillment of God's magnanimous promises to Abraham. Isaac was the elect son, the chosen one.

Then is the unchosen one rejected? Abandoned? Cursed?

No. The promise God gives to one does not imply a curse on others, any more than rain can give its nourishment to one plant while withholding it from others. God's good gifts overflow and there is no hint of stinginess in his blessing.

"Oh that Ishmael might live before you!"

The response – translated "No, but Sarah your wife shall bear you a son" – should not be understood as God's rejection of Abraham's request but as God's correction of his expectation.[3] Ultimately, Abraham's request was honored by God. Ishmael was blessed and multiplied. He would father twelve princes – not unlike Isaac's future son, Jacob – and he would also be a great nation. We read the fulfillment of that promise later in the Genesis narrative where the twelve princes are listed by name and their dwelling place is also described as "over against all his kinsmen." A promise kept.

God also gave Abraham a physical sign to enact, as a statement of his faith in God's promise. The males of his household were to be circumcised as a sign of the covenant made by God. Though the primitive nature of the story and this bloody sign of promise may offend our sensibilities, we must not let the significance of the enactment escape us. It is a sign in human flesh of belonging, first to God and then to the family of Abraham.

Abraham was not one to dither concerning God's promises. That very day, all the males of his household were circumcised.

That very day, Abraham and his son Ishmael were circumcised.

Abraham loved the boy. He would become a great nation, established from twelve noble chieftains. If that's not enough to view this young man in a different light, consider that Ishmael was likely the first person to receive the

---

3. Maalouf, *Arabs in the Shadow of Israel*, 82.

sign of God's covenant in his flesh. Such a thing would hardly be said of one who turned away from God or of one whom God rejected.

"Oh that Ishmael might live before you!"

You are Ishmael. I am Ishmael. We are not of that designated line of promise that brought the Messiah's blessing to all the nations of the world. But we are the ones on whom it has spilled over – those brought into the covenant even though we were born outside the line of promise. We, along with Ishmael, have experienced an adoption, a grafting into the chosen line, such that Abraham has truly become the father of a multitude of nations.

Yes, of course, I am Ishmael.

11

Laughter

The LORD visited Sarah as he had said, and the LORD did to Sarah as he had promised. And Sarah conceived and bore Abraham a son in his old age at the time of which God had spoken to him. Abraham called the name of his son who was born to him, whom Sarah bore him, Isaac. And Abraham circumcised his son Isaac when he was eight days old, as God had commanded him. Abraham was a hundred years old when his son Isaac was born to him. And Sarah said, "God has made laughter for me; everyone who hears will laugh over me." And she said, "Who would have said to Abraham that Sarah would nurse children? Yet I have borne him a son in his old age." (Genesis 21:1–7)

And the child grew and was weaned. And Abraham made a great feast on the day that Isaac was weaned. But Sarah saw the son of Hagar the Egyptian, whom she had borne to Abraham, laughing. So she said to Abraham, "Cast out this slave woman with her son, for the son of this slave woman shall not be heir with my son Isaac." And the thing was very displeasing to Abraham on account of his son. But God said to Abraham, "Be not displeased because of the boy and because of your slave woman. Whatever Sarah says to you, do as she tells you, for through Isaac shall your offspring be named. And I will make a nation of the son of the slave woman also, because he is your offspring." (Genesis 21:8–13)

63

64

Laughter . . .

To think it was his laughter that landed Ishmael in such trouble. Her son's name is laughter! What!? Can only one son be happy? Can only one boy express joy and delight? Could not my son also be a son of laughter?

All these years I've submitted under her hand, just like the angel told me. Now, one mistake – a boy's laughter – and we're out!

I've watched this whole thing unfold and unravel.

I never dreamed mistress Sarah would have a baby. Abraham said it would happen. He said it was God's promise. Still, to have a baby at her age seemed impossible. But now it's real. It happened.

Ishmael is out. Isaac is in.

Tomorrow we leave. God only knows where we will go.

Despite all this mess, I search my mind and the memories give me hope. The angel told me that Ishmael would be a free man, that he would resist slavery, that he would be a great nation.

Ishmael's laughter is the cause of my misfortune. But it may also be the end of my slavery. I choose to hold the angel's promises in my heart and live for them, just like I've seen Abraham do. Also, I could see it in his eyes – he doesn't want to let his son go. His heart is with Ishmael. Ishmael's path may be rough, but he has had a father and has known a father's love. And for that I am grateful.

It is an ironic literary twist that laughter takes on such importance in the birth and naming of Isaac. When Abraham was first told that Sarah would bear him a child, he literally fell on his face and laughed. It is difficult for the contemporary reader to understand what is going on here. Is Abraham laughing in disbelief? I think not. First, he is not one to disbelieve God's promises, and God does not censure his disbelief as he does Sarah's.

Perhaps this is the laughter of resignation, as if to say, "OK. When this happens, I'll have seen it all!" Abraham has heard these promises more than once. He has found a solution for his lack of an heir – Ishmael. So now he has moved on. It's as though he doesn't wish to revisit the painful problem of Sarah's infertility. Yet, the divine visitor is not content to move on. He insists that the promised heir will come through Sarah.

In response to Abraham's laughter, God names the son of promise "Isaac," literally "he laughs."

It's not only Abraham who laughs. In the next chapter, the divine visitor makes his way to Abraham's tent yet again and receives Abraham's generous hospitality.

During this eventful visit, Yahweh promises Abraham that he will visit again in about a year's time and that Sarah will have borne a son. Sarah, who is eavesdropping, laughs when she overhears this: "So Sarah laughed to herself, saying, 'After I am worn out, and my lord is old, shall I have pleasure?'" The narrator fills in the details, letting the reader know that Sarah is past childbearing years: "the way of women had ceased to be with Sarah." The visitor, knowing that Sarah is overhearing the conversation asks, "Why did Sarah laugh and say 'Shall I indeed bear a child now that I am old?' Is anything too hard for Yahweh?"[1] Sarah's laughter expresses her incredulity at such a preposterous idea – a ninety-year-old woman having a baby!

So there's been plenty of laughter to go around. The laughter of disbelief on the part of Sarah and the laughter of resignation on the part of Abraham, but all of that is redeemed in the naming of the newborn son. Sarah declares "God has made laughter for me; everyone who hears will laugh over me." Sarah's good fortune will be the occasion of joyful laughter on the part of those who hear.

I suggest that it is not mere coincidence that Ishmael is cast out because of his laughter. Laughter takes place in the narrative for a variety of reasons, but all of it is occasioned by the miraculous birth of this unexpected son.

There have been attempts to read derision or scorn into Ishmael's laughter. Perhaps Sarah's irritation owes to a disparaging tone in Ishmael's mirth.

---

1. Genesis 18:11–14.

However, the text gives no indication of that. Furthermore, Abraham's grief over the situation, coupled with God's subsequent hearing of Ishmael's cry, suggests that the laughter was innocent.

If the age of Isaac at his weaning was three, we may assume the young Ishmael was in his mid-teens. It is certainly possible that the older boy was having fun at young Isaac's expense, but the text, taken at face value, simply indicates that Ishmael's laughter incited Sarah's protective instinct. She demands that the "son of the slave woman" be cast out so as not to threaten the inheritance of Isaac.

Abraham receives direction from the Lord to act upon Sarah's request even though it was "very displeasing" or "very grievous" to him. Before Ishmael and his mother are cast out, the Lord reaffirms his promise that Ishmael will also be a great nation, since he too is Abraham's son.

Laughter was the occasion of Ishmael's expulsion. Under Sarah's roof, only one child could be the son of laughter. Sarah's demand portrays the distance she wishes to place between her son and Ishmael. Twice she refers to "this slave woman" and "her son."[2]

The story portrays the affection of Abraham for Ishmael, and we may discern in that fatherly love a reflection of God's love towards the young Ishmael and his mother. Ishmael's laughter meets with Sarah's displeasure, but not God's. Sarah's fear leads to the pair's expulsion despite the grief it caused Abraham. However, Sarah's fear will not determine Ishmael's destiny. It is merely the instrument through which God brings about his good purposes for the young man.

Isaac will be Abraham's heir and through him will come the fulfillment of God's promises in the Messiah. Nevertheless, God's promises do not exclude Ishmael and his mother. Though cast out of Abraham's home, they move on towards a destiny granted them by the love of a heavenly Father.

---

2. Maalouf, *Arabs in the Shadow of Israel*, 91.

12

God Hears

*So Abraham rose early in the morning and took bread and a
skin of water and gave it to Hagar, putting it on her shoulder,
along with the child, and sent her away. And she departed and
wandered in the wilderness of Beersheba. (Genesis 21:14)*

*When the water in the skin was gone, she put the child under one of
the bushes. Then she went and sat down opposite him a good way
off, about the distance of a bowshot, for she said, "Let me not look
on the death of the child." And as she sat opposite him, she lifted up
her voice and wept. And God heard the voice of the boy, and the
angel of God called to Hagar from heaven and said to her, "What
troubles you, Hagar? Fear not, for God has heard the voice of the
boy where he is. Up! Lift up the boy, and hold him fast with your
hand, for I will make him into a great nation." Then God opened her
eyes, and she saw a well of water. And she went and filled the skin
with water and gave the boy a drink. And God was with the boy,
and he grew up. He lived in the wilderness and became an expert
with the bow. He lived in the wilderness of Paran, and his mother
took a wife for him from the land of Egypt. (Genesis 21:15–21)*

One skin of water under this scorching sun. Master should have known it wouldn't last. Maybe he knew.

I have no idea where to go or who will take us in.
Ishmael's growing limp. He's big now. I can't carry him any further, and even if I could, I don't know where I'm going. How could it come to this? It's been hours, and it feels like I'm wandering in circles.

This is what Sarah wanted after all – to be rid of Ishmael, nothing standing in the way of her son. And where does that leave me? Leave Ishmael?
His skin is shriveling up. (She hears him moaning through parched throat and lips.) There's no shade in this Godforsaken place.

Here – let me get him under this bush. Is there no one to help? I can't see!
Get me away. I can't look. Please, no!

Abraham's acts of obedience, which have bitter implications for the old patriarch, often take place in the early hours of the morning. Abraham rises early to obey God's command. He sends Hagar off with her son – *his* son.

In light of the extreme deprivation that mother and son endure, Abraham's preparations seem thoughtless, utterly inadequate. A skin of water hoisted onto Hagar's shoulder is hardly adequate provision for a desert journey with no specific destination. The rabbis, perhaps embarrassed by the patriarch's apparent miserliness, explained that Hagar and Ishmael were sinners, who could not be permitted to stay in the same household with the righteous Abraham. They saw further justification in structural parallels between the story of Hagar being sent out and the story of Adam's banishment after his act of disobedience.[1]

Judging from Hagar's predicament, the rabbis might have been right. After a period of time, she reaches the point of utter despair. Those who have experienced the intense heat of the desert know the feeling. There is no recourse against the merciless desert sun. The body simply cannot withstand its assault.

Unlike the road to Shur, the wilderness of Beersheba has no natural water source. We may imagine that the desert journey left this young mother in a state of shock, reeling from the reality that she and her son are now cut off from Abraham as a result of Sarah's fear.

There was only one way that Abraham could demonstrate that Ishmael had no claim on the inheritance. He had to set Hagar free. In doing so, the slave's son would give up any claim to the family property. This is Sarah's demand, with which Abraham reluctantly complies. In fact, Abraham's consternation at the thought of losing his son may allow the reader's imagination to envision a harsh exchange that may have taken place between the aged couple before the Lord intervened to confirm Sarah's directives.[2]

It is ironic that though Hagar may have hoped for freedom many times before, her receiving it now holds only the promise of misery and desolation. The bond Ishmael shared with his father is painfully shattered. The boy's comforts, not to mention his future security, are withdrawn. The youth who stands on the threshold of manhood is pushed over prematurely.

Wandering in the wilderness is a recurrent theme in the Hebrew Bible. Joseph and the children of Israel will also face the threat of death in the wilderness. It is a theatre of vulnerability – a place where one either meets

---

1. Aryeh Cohen, "Hagar and Ishmael: A Commentary," *Interpretation: A Journal of Bible and Theology* 68, no. 3 (2014): 251.

2. Maalouf, *Arabs in the Shadow of Israel*, 91–92.

one's end or one's God. It stands in contrast to creation – the ordering of existence – as a place of chaos, insecurity and destruction.[3] So, in the wilderness of Beersheba, the child is laid to rest. Hagar "flings" (a more literal reading than "puts") her son under a bush and takes up her position opposite him – a bowshot away. The note of irony and redemption could hardly be more pronounced. Ishmael, now lying helpless in the chaotic wilderness, will soon master his hostile surroundings. He will be the consummate desert hunter, an expert with the bow and a survivalist. His desert debut and his mother's despair provide the austere backdrop foreshadowing a redeemed destiny.

It is here, surrounded by desert, with death silently stealing upon her and her young son, that Hagar lifts up her voice and weeps. She has positioned herself so as "not to see" the death of her son. The former encounter at the well on the way to Shur was punctuated with "seeing." Hagar was seen by God and also saw him. In contrast, her inability to see the water source and her unwillingness to see her son's death portray profound despair. As her seeing in the earlier episode was life and renewal, her non-seeing here depicts death.[4]

Hagar weeps. God hears. It is the same phrase that is used when God hears the cry of the Israelites while they are under the oppressive domination of the pharaohs.[5]

"What troubles you, Hagar?" It is the first time her name is called independently of her status as servant of Sarah. The question is even more sparing in words than our translation renders it: "What's with you, Hagar?" The divine interrogation might well assault our sense of decency. She is in desperate straits, having resigned herself to her son's death as he lies prostrate beneath a desert shrub. God's unconscionable question confronts a bewildered mother as it confronts us.

"Up! Lift up the boy, and hold him fast with your hand." The last time she heard the divine voice, she was told to submit herself under the hand of a mistress who had only recently abused her. The Lord who had placed her under Sarah's hand now places her hand under Ishmael to uphold him. Her own hand will revive the boy to fulfill his God-appointed destiny.

In a strikingly beautiful declaration, the divine voice reminds Hagar of the name given to her son years earlier on the road to Shur – Ishmael, "God has heard the voice of the boy where he is." She knew where he was. It was her despair that had led her to fling him under a desert bush. Could there be

---

3. Cohen, "Hagar and Ishmael: A Commentary," 252.

4. Spitzer, "Where Do You Come From," 13.

5. Exodus 2:24.

a more isolated and Godforsaken environment? Yet, the voice of the boy was heard by God. Ishmael. God hears. He has not forgotten and he will bring about what he has promised: "I will make him into a great nation." Hagar's delicate support of her son of promise mirrors the care of Yahweh who held Israel by the hand as he led his people out of Egypt.[6]

With divine assistance, Hagar is able to see a well. As seeing returns to Hagar, life and renewal return to the story. The boy revives, and God is with him. Though our modern ears are liable to pass over the succinct declaration with scarce notice, we must pause. Ishmael is not the promised son; he is not the son of Sarah, but the son of Hagar. Yet his birth came with great promise, which was now being fulfilled as God hears the boy's voice and intervenes to save him. In few words, the ancient text bursts forth with meaning and hope – "I will make him into a great nation."[7] Though the son has left the house of Abraham, the God of Abraham has not left his son. It is a gospel declaration of God's favor lavished on one outside the bounds of the promise. Such a promise sustains hope even in the most desperate moment.

---

6. Jeremiah 31:32.
7. Genesis 17:20.

13

Son of the Slave

Tell me, you who desire to be under the law, do you not listen to the law? For it is written that Abraham had two sons, one by a slave woman and one by a free woman. But the son of the slave was born according to the flesh, while the son of the free woman was born through promise. Now this may be interpreted allegorically: these women are two covenants. One is from Mount Sinai, bearing children for slavery; she is Hagar. Now Hagar is Mount Sinai in Arabia; she corresponds to the present Jerusalem, for she is in slavery with her children. But the Jerusalem above is free, and she is our mother. For it is written,

"Rejoice, O barren one who does not bear;
break forth and cry aloud, you who are not in labor!
For the children of the desolate one will be more
than those of the one who has a husband."

Now you, brothers, like Isaac, are children of promise. But just as at that time he who was born according to the flesh persecuted him who was born according to the Spirit, so also it is now. But what does the Scripture say? "Cast out the slave woman and her son, for the son of the slave woman shall not inherit with the son of the free woman." So, brothers, we are not children of the slave but of the free woman. (Galatians 4:21–31)

Mediterranean Sea

Red Sea

N

Much contemporary preaching and writing assumes that Ishmael's lot in life is slavery and persecution of Israel. Many modern students of the Bible are so far removed from the peoples and cultures of the Near East that this assumption is accepted without question. Ishmael is viewed as a source of animosity and antagonism to the seed of Abraham. His wild, "donkey-like" character is portrayed in the worst possible light – a source of obstinacy and stupidity, a true beast of burden. "His hand against everyone and everyone's hand against him." What could this imply other than the sad reality of centuries of inveterate warfare among the peoples of the Near East?

As we have seen, the widely-read New International Version translated the place of Ishmael's dwelling as expressing this entrenched enmity: "he will live in hostility toward all his brothers."[1] But subsequent chapters of Genesis bear out the literal meaning that Ishmael was not to live among his brothers, but opposite and separate from them. No hostility need be implied.

The understanding of the promises to Ishmael portrayed in this book challenges these popular assumptions and seeks to cast Hagar and Ishmael in a truer light. We are asking the same questions Jesus posed to the expert in Old Testament law: "What is written in the Law?" and "How do you read it?"[2] Concerning Hagar and Ishmael, *what* does it say and *how* do we read it? What is the lens through which we look at this text and how does that clarify or skew what is actually written?

We will return to the Old Testament story, but first we must visit Paul's analogy of Hagar and Sarah as it has become the singular lens through which many view Ishmael.

Whether consciously or unconsciously, Paul's allegory based on Sarah and Hagar contributes to our expectation of enmity between Ishmael and Isaac. In Galatians 4, the apostle draws from the story of Hagar and Sarah to make an application in his own day, to the reality which is dawning in the early church.

Paul had frequently encountered the issue of ongoing Jewish adherence to the Mosaic law. His visit to Jerusalem (Acts 21) revealed a profound loyalty to the law of Moses, both among Jewish believers in Christ and among the general Jewish population. After arriving in Jerusalem, Paul and his companions informed the apostles of what God had accomplished among the Gentiles. They (James and the elders) glorified God on this account and also shared with Paul "how many thousands there are among the Jews of those who have believed."[3]

---

1. Genesis 16:12.
2. Luke 10:26.
3. Acts 21:20.

Here was the issue: these Jewish believers, though they had embraced Christ, were also zealous for the Mosaic law. The Gentiles who had believed, on the contrary, had little inclination to embrace the Old Testament regulations. The apostles had already dealt with this issue in the Jerusalem Council of Acts 15, but it was not going away, especially not in Jerusalem. The new wine of the gospel, in its forward movement among non-Jewish peoples, appeared to be bursting the old wineskin of adherence to the Mosaic law. What should be done?

In fact, the two were not contradictory. Jesus was the in-flesh fulfillment of God's Torah – his wise teaching on how humanity should live and conduct its affairs. His teaching soared to new heights and called his followers to obey the law of God from a transformed heart brought about by the indwelling Holy Spirit. Nevertheless, the outworking of releasing the old and embracing the new was proving to be a challenge.

The issue of adherence to the Mosaic law pops up in the churches which Paul and his companions had labored to plant in Asia Minor. And so, in his letter to the Galatians, Paul employs an analogy to explain the relation of the law to the gospel. Paul writes, "the heir, as long as he is a child, is no different from a slave, though he is the owner of everything, but he is under guardians and managers until the date set by his father." A minor child, like a slave, remains under the supervision of guardians and managers. When the son comes of age, he is then free from guardians and managers. He moves into the freedom and authority of his position as son. This son represents the Jewish people, who have lived under the tutelage of the law but are now free to step into their authoritative role as sons and daughters. The transfer from servant to son is likened to the transfer from adherence to the Mosaic law to adoption as sons through the indwelling Spirit.

Paul then shifts from analogy to allegory, although the imagery of sonship and freedom from the law remains the core issue. The son of the slave woman, says Paul, is the one "born according to the flesh," born through human ingenuity and planning. This imagery would connect with Paul's hearers, who were well aware of the story of Sarai's attempt to secure an heir for Abraham and were familiar with God's declaration that Isaac – a son born through God's intervention – was the promised seed.

So those who insist on adherence to the Mosaic law are like the son of Hagar. They rely on human effort to bring about God's promise, which can never be effected through human planning and implementation. God's promise comes to fruition despite human ingenuity and beyond it. "Through Sarah will your seed come." Through Christ the promises of God are "yes" and "amen."

It is the promise of God, expressed in Christ alone that saves, not adherence to the law.

At a given moment, God sent forth his Son "born of woman, born under the law, to redeem those who were under the law, so that we might receive adoption as sons." Christ is the son of the promise. His appearance inaugurates our adoption, whether Jews or Gentiles, as bona fide sons and daughters with full rights in the family. He is the Isaac of the new covenant in whom all the nations of the earth, both Jews and Gentiles, will be blessed. As Paul had said earlier, those who are of faith are the sons of Abraham.[4] Clearly, sonship is not enacted by living under the law, under the tutelage of the Mosaic stipulations. It is a new reality, a coming of age, whereby all who are in Christ step into the freedom and authority of sons and daughters.

If the analogy is understood properly, it says nothing about the physical descendants of Ishmael. Ironically, it is the recalcitrant sons of Isaac – those who insist on adherence to the law and allegiance to the earthly Jerusalem, and refuse to recognize in Christ the fulfillment of God's promise – who are the "son of the slave woman."

If we are to rightly divide God's word, it is important to note that this analogy does not concern a particular ethnic group in the Middle East today – whether Jews or Gentiles. It is allegorically applied to those who insisted on adherence to the Mosaic law *along* with faith in Christ in the time of the apostles. It should not be understood to perpetuate longstanding enmities among the peoples of today's Near East. Such an understanding would not only perpetuate an ethnic superiority of one group over another but make a travesty of Christ's divine law to love one's neighbor as oneself.

A further difficult issue arises from the Galatians passage. Paul states that the son of the slave woman "persecuted" the son of the promise. We have examined this "persecution," which was likely nothing more than a naughty laugh of a thirteen-year-old boy at his younger brother. Sarah's preoccupation with Isaac's inheritance was the more likely culprit for Ishmael's expulsion. Nevertheless, Paul draws out his analogy by applying it to the persecution Christ-followers (both Jews and Gentiles) were experiencing at the hands of the Jews who resisted the new wine of Christ's gospel.

Though Paul does make this allegorical application, it is unfair to read a longstanding persecution back into the Ishmael-Isaac relationship. The apostle is drawing on a known story and events to provide perspective as to why persecution is taking place among the Galatians at that point in history. The

---

4. Galatians 3:7.

use of this analogy does not dispense with the need for careful study of the Old Testament in its own context.

As the church ventures into the twenty-first century, with all its crises and challenges, it is imperative that we reexamine the Hagar and Ishmael story. Given Paul's passion for the unfolding mystery of the gospel – that, in Christ, the nations are coheirs with the physical descendants of Abraham – we would be guilty of misreading the Bible if we understood Paul to commend an ethnic bias inherent in God's grace and election. Paul is not fencing ethnic Arabs outside of God's redemptive love and grace, nor is he excluding his own kinsmen, the Jews. Quite the contrary. Paul is expounding the gospel of freedom which welcomes all – Jew and Gentile – into the family of God as brothers and sisters.

Martin Luther's treatment of Paul's allegory may serve as a guide. He suggests that what Hagar symbolized for the apostle Paul is a different reality than who she was historically. The Pauline allegory presents a different truth than the Genesis narrative of Hagar. Both are equally inspired of God, addressing different situations and calling for different responses.[5]

So how do *you* read this story? What lens are you using? Is Ishmael still the source of perpetual enmity, a wild and obstinate beast of burden? The matter is significant. Finding Hagar may depend on how Christ's body perceives Ishmael. We will return to this issue in a subsequent chapter, but as we turn, in the next chapter, to the simple burial scene of the father of our faith, it may be a good place for us to symbolically bury our misconception of his eldest son and his mother.

5. John L. Thompson, "Hagar, Victim or Villain? Three Sixteenth-Century Views," *The Catholic Biblical Quarterly* 59 (1997): 230.

14

Progeny

These are the days of the years of Abraham's life, 175 years. Abraham breathed his last and died in a good old age, an old man and full of years, and was gathered to his people. Isaac and Ishmael his sons buried him in the cave of Machpelah, in the field of Ephron the son of Zohar the Hittite, east of Mamre, the field that Abraham purchased from the Hittites. There Abraham was buried, with Sarah his wife. After the death of Abraham, God blessed Isaac his son. And Isaac settled at Beer-lahai-roi. (Genesis 26:7–11)

These are the generations of Ishmael, Abraham's son, whom Hagar the Egyptian, Sarah's servant, bore to Abraham. These are the names of the sons of Ishmael, named in the order of their birth: Nebaioth, the firstborn of Ishmael; and Kedar, Adbeel, Mibsam, Mishma, Dumah, Massa, Hadad, Tema, Jetur, Naphish, and Kedemah. These are the sons of Ishmael and these are their names, by their villages and by their encampments, twelve princes according to their tribes. (These are the years of the life of Ishmael: 137 years. He breathed his last and died, and was gathered to his people.) They settled from Havilah to Shur, which is opposite Egypt in the direction of Assyria. He settled over against all his kinsmen. (Genesis 26:12–18)

Hagar is never heard from again. She disappears behind the curtains of the Hebrew drama as quickly as she appeared. By the time Abraham was buried, Hagar, if still alive, may have been nearing 110 years of age. The story continues through Isaac, his son Jacob and the twelve tribes of Israel. Ishmael and his mother played a limited role for a brief moment in time. The biblical narrative will unfold, largely disinterested in the people of Ishmael – though we will soon discover that they do not entirely vanish.

The next appearance of Ishmael is in the company of his brother Isaac, at the burial of their father Abraham. The portrayal of the patriarch's death is peaceful, expressing a full and contented life. He is of a "good old age" – a description of his gray hair. He was "full" or "satisfied" in years and "gathered to his people."

"Gathered to his people" is an interesting phrase, used in reference to the deaths of several Old Testament saints. It is noteworthy that Ishmael also makes this list, in the company of Isaac, Jacob, Aaron and Moses. A Jewish commentator observes that this phrase

> testifies to a belief that, despite his mortality and perishability, man possesses an immortal element that survives the loss of life. Death is looked upon as a transition to an afterlife where one is united with one's ancestors. This interpretation contradicts the widespread, but apparently erroneous view that such a notion is unknown in Israel until later times.[1]

These words indicate that Yahweh's blessing rested on Ishmael as it did on his father, Abraham. He died in peace and was gathered to his ancestors, among them, Abraham.

The presence of both sons at Abraham's burial should not be passed over. Abraham had six other sons through Keturah[2] – but as far as we know, none of them are present at the burial. We may surmise that Ishmael's presence at this final juncture indicates the mutual affection between father and son. For thirteen years, prior to his traumatic expulsion, Ishmael was an only son. Now, eighty-nine years later, Ishmael himself is an aged patriarch. Both he and Isaac can look back on events with the maturity of age and the realization that God's sovereign hand was orchestrating events. The sting of that expulsion during his teen years, like an ebbing tide, has faded, and a paternal bond has been reestablished. In this moving scene, there is no hint of contention between

---

1. Sarna, *Genesis*, 175.

2. Genesis 25:1–2. We will consider the Jewish Rabbis' views that Keturah was actually Hagar in a later chapter.

Ishmael and Isaac. Abraham's past is acknowledged as he is gathered to his ancestors. The burial also points to his ongoing and future influence through the two sons – his progeny.

Isaac settles at Beer-lahai-roi. The well took its name from Hagar's encounter with the God who "sees me." The son of promise does not disown the locale or play down its significance. Hagar's "finding" is apparently cherished in the collective family memory, anticipating further fraternal interaction among Abraham's progeny. Isaac is content to live through the provision of "the well of the living one who sees me" – the name given to the well by Hagar.

The naming of Ishmael's twelve sons deserves our attention. They parallel the twelve tribes of Israel who will be born to Jacob, the younger of Isaac's twin sons. More importantly, the author of Genesis is keen to demonstrate God's generous response to Abraham's prayer, "Oh that Ishmael might live before you!" The promise of twelve princes or chieftains issuing from Ishmael is first heard in Genesis 17 in response to Abraham's plea; now, on the occasion of Abraham's death, the twelve are named.

It is worth noting that the sons of Ishmael are not portrayed as Israel's inveterate enemies as many presume. Rather, they are spoken of from time to time in the biblical narrative as tribes who, after enduring the Lord's discipline,[3] will join in the worship of Israel's Messiah King. The following paragraphs survey some of these biblical mentions of Ishmael's line.[4]

Jeremiah looks with astonishment on Israel and declares that envoys should be sent as far as Kedar to inquire whether a nation has ever changed its god as has Israel by forsaking her living waters for broken cisterns.[5] It seems that Kedar became symbolic of those dwelling in the East as Ezekiel also associates Arabia with Kedar's princes (Ezek 27:21). Isaiah 60:1–7 describes how the Messiah will unite the scattered family of Abraham in his light. The two elder sons of Ishmael are mentioned among the nations that contribute their wealth and livestock to the service of the Messiah.

---

3. See Isaiah 21:16–17 and Jeremiah 49:28–33 as examples of God's cleansing judgment on Kedar. David also bemoaned his dwelling among the tents of Kedar in Psalm 120:5.

4. See Maalouf, *Arabs in the Shadow of Israel*, 151 for historical and archaeological evidence of the twelve tribes of Ishmael. Maalouf points out that attempts have been made to identify Nabaioth with the Nabateans whose capitol was Petra in southern Jordan. Though this suggestion has merit, it cannot be relied upon fully due to orthographical dissimilarities between Nabaioth and Nabatea in Semitic languages (151). Others suggest that the Nabateans originated with the tribe of Kedar, son of Ishmael.

Unpublished notes by Dr. Paul Blackham on Abraham, Hagar and Ishmael, were also helpful in assessing the progeny of Ishmael.

5. See Jeremiah 2:10–12.

Arise, shine, for your light has come, and the glory of the LORD rises upon you. See, darkness covers the earth and thick darkness is over the peoples, but the LORD rises upon you and his glory appears over you. Nations will come to your light, and kings to the brightness of your dawn . . . Herds of camels will cover your land, young camels of Midian and Ephah. And all from Sheba will come, bearing gold and incense and proclaiming the praise of the LORD. All *Kedar's* flocks will be gathered to you, the rams of *Nebaioth* will serve you; they will be accepted as offerings on my altar, and I will adorn my glorious temple.

Isaiah 42 is a renowned and beautiful Old Testament depiction of the ministry of the Messiah as a covenant for the peoples and a light for the nations. Matthew quotes this prophecy at length to describe the Spirit-anointed Christ who proclaims justice to the nations through his gentle leadership: "A bruised reed he will not break and a smoldering wick he will not quench until he brings justice to victory" (Matt 12:20). The descendants of Ishmael are included as those who benefit from the benevolent rule of Messiah. "Let the desert and its cities lift up their voice, the villages that *Kedar* inhabits." (Isa 42:11a). God intends to fulfill his promises to Abraham through the blessing of Messiah on his eldest son – Ishmael – as they "sing to the LORD a new song, his praise from the end of the earth" (Isa 42:10a).

There is an intriguing oracle addressed to *Dumah* in Isaiah 21:11–12: "An oracle concerning Dumah: One is calling to me from Seir, 'Watchman, what time of the night? Watchman, what time of the night?' The watchman says, 'Morning comes, and also the night. If you will inquire, come back again.'"

In this enigmatic prophecy, the Ishmaelite tribe repeatedly seeks understanding from the Lord's prophet concerning the dark times in which they live. The prophetic response is that the dawn is coming, even though it will be followed by another night of trouble. Yet they are to return to consult the prophet again. We can surmise that the prophet held out hope for these Ishmaelites who sought divine light through the prophetic word.

A point of interest is that the names of two of Ishmael's sons are repeated in the list of the sons of Simeon (one of Jacob's twelve sons). Mibsam (literally "fragrance") and Mishma (literally "hearing") are found in both lists of sons. It is possible that these were two pairs of separate individuals; however, some suggest that these two sons of Ishmael were united to the Israelite tribe of Simeon. Might this unexpected merging of Isaac and Ishmael express fraternal and peaceful relations rather than the often presumed enmity between the two?

Finally, the tribe of *Massa* is the origin of the Masanoi – a north Arabian tribe which produced the sages Lemuel and Agur who authored Proverbs chapters 30 and 31.[6] Surprisingly, Ishmael's descendants were included among the authors of the biblical wisdom literature.

Speaking of wisdom literature, Job is described as "greatest of all the people of the East" (Job 1:3). This designation refers to the nomads of the Syro-Arabian Desert, whom Jeremiah linked with Kedar, the son of Ishmael (Jer 49:28). An Aramaic tradition links Job with Jobab (mentioned in Genesis 36:33), a descendant of Esau who married Basma, the daughter of Ishmael. Although we cannot be certain about this tradition, we know that Job was not from the line of Isaac.[7]

God's election of Isaac does not entail his rejection of Ishmael. Isaac was the promised seed through whom the Messiah would come. However, the line of the chosen seed did not exhaust the grace of God and thereby deprive the surrounding peoples and nations of his blessing. Though the biblical story does not focus on the twelve sons of Ishmael, there are indicators that God continued to bless the eldest son of Abraham in his land.

In the grand sweep of the biblical narrative, it is a grave mistake to assume that Ishmael became the chronic enemy of God's chosen people. The biblical evidence simply does not support it.

---

6. Maalouf, *Arabs in the Shadow of Israel*, 154.
7. Maalouf, *Arabs in the Shadow of Israel*, 121–124.

15

Considering Hagar and Moses

I think about it so often – how the Lord told me to take up that boy and put my hand behind his head and give him water to drink.

I really thought it was all over. Ishmael looked like he was almost gone – parched lips, gaunt cheeks, heartrending groans fading into tired whimpers. I knew that limp little body couldn't hold on to life much longer . . .

And yet, there was a well. How did I not see it? To this day I don't know if it was there and I just didn't see it or if the Lord suddenly planted it there.

How did all this happen?
To this day it baffles me that God used me to save Ishmael. And to think that my son, Hagar's son, will become a prince and father of a great nation! I can hardly take it all in. I loved that boy more than life itself, but I was at my wit's end. My heart had given up hope. I know it was really the Lord who saved him, and yet – strangely, amazingly, excitingly – it was also me. It was me just doing exactly what he told me to do.

Yes, he lifts up the lowly and exalts this woman of low degree!

W e have been trying to get a different vision of Hagar, to understand her not as a cursed and excluded woman, but as a daughter of Yahweh, a blessed mother of a great nation. Now you are invited to take one more step in reenvisioning Hagar and understanding her as an Old Testament precursor of the gospel – and as an outsider who is deeply loved and honored, and blessed through God's grace alone, which leads her to an obedient response of faith.

In brief, we are going to consider elements of Hagar's life that parallel that of Moses. Recognizing that parallel structure should help us see that the author of the first five books of the Bible must have viewed Hagar as a great woman of God. If he had not, he would never have intentionally paralleled her life with that of Moses – one of the greatest prophets of God, the giver of the law and the rescuer of Israel.

In order to understand this parallel between Moses and Hagar, it will help to be aware of some recent developments in biblical studies. The Bible is literature. In fact, it is a library – a collection of ancient writings – which fit together to tell a unified story. This single plot line is not always evident to a casual observer. Nevertheless, it is there, and it is always pointing us forward to the culmination of the biblical story in Jesus Christ.

As literature, the Bible should be read observing its literary features – character, plot, setting, etc. The Bible is not primarily a religious textbook, giving precise information; nor is it an instruction manual, telling us what to do and what to avoid doing. These elements are frequently present, but, as literature, the Bible invites us to observe and contemplate its characters and especially their interactions with God. As we study the characters of Hagar and Moses, along with the themes that animated their life and faith, we will see that both are held up as examples of godliness and grace whom God used to save and secure a future for themselves and for their descendants.

By comparing the lives of Hagar and Moses, we will observe several points of commonality between the two characters. Both endure intense family conflict – which was a central factor in their faith and calling. Both display similar traits and behaviors. Both journey into the wilderness and encounter God there, leading to their transformation and a vision for their futures. Finally, both Hagar and Moses become founders of a new and blessed nation.[1] Now let's look more closely at these commonalities.

---

1. Thomas B. Dozeman, "The Wilderness and Salvation History in the Hagar Story," *Journal of Biblical Literature* 117.1 (1998): 23–43. I am indebted to Dozeman and his article for the content of this chapter which follows his work very closely, as I could do little to improve on his informative study.

Hagar's unique calling resulted from her dual status as the surrogate wife of Abraham and mother of his heir and as Sarah's slave girl. This dual status leads to family conflict that comes to a head in Sarah's insistence that Hagar and her son leave the household of Abraham.

Moses also had a dual identity – he was the adopted son of Pharaoh's daughter and also one of the oppressed Hebrews. As with Hagar, this double identity led to an intense conflict with Pharaoh, the king of Egypt. Like Hagar, Moses flees into the wilderness to escape the threat of death.

The flight of both characters leads to a series of events that shape their future and calling. First, there is an encounter with God in the wilderness. Second, both characters are commanded to return to the perilous situation from which they have fled. Finally, both Hagar and Moses receive a promise from God and leave the wilderness with a new understanding of God, which is expressed in a new name for God. Hagar names God "El-Ro'ï" – "The Seeing One" or "The One Who Sees Me." Moses, on the other hand, receives a revelation of God's name, Yahweh – "I AM."

The parallels continue as both Hagar and Moses return to take up new roles in response to God's revelation. Hagar returns to be the wife of Abraham and mother of his firstborn son, Ishmael; Moses returns to Egypt, together with his brother Aaron, as a liberator of the Hebrew people. These new roles produce yet more conflict for both Hagar and Moses, resulting in their being cast out and returning once more to the wilderness. Though the expulsions are cruel for Hagar and Moses (and the Israelites), both are sanctioned by God. God instructs Abraham to listen to Sarah and send Hagar and Ishmael away (Gen 21:11–12); Moses is informed by God that Pharaoh will cast the Israelites out (Exod 11:1). Both expulsions are acts of liberation from slavery – Hagar is released from her bondage to Sarah; Moses and the Israelites are released from the oppression of Egypt.

Though both are freed from enslavement, the struggle has not ended, as both Hagar and Moses must now face the immense challenges posed by life in the wilderness. The wilderness had once been a place of escape from oppression, but now it poses a constant threat to the well-being of Hagar and Ishmael, as well as Moses and the nation of Israel. Perhaps we have a foreshadowing of this threat in that both Hagar and the Israelites are portrayed as taking meager provisions such as could be carried on their shoulders (Gen 21:14; Exod 12:34). A lack of water threatens those they care for – Ishmael is near death from thirst while Israel's water source is contaminated (Exod 15:24).

Both characters are responsible for the well-being of others – Hagar is the mother of Ishmael while Moses is the deliverer of the Hebrew people. Moreover, both characters intercede in dire circumstances for God's intervention to save those for whom they are responsible. God indeed acts to save his people, but what is perhaps even more instructive is that God's saving acts are also accompanied by further revelation of his character based on the previous revelation of his name. In the case of Hagar, God is the one who hears the boy's cry, recalling his naming of Ishmael. Concerning Moses, God instructs him to purify the water and then reveals that he is Yahweh, the healer of the people (Exod 15:25–26).

The purification of the water by Moses leads to yet another point of connection between the stories of Hagar and Moses. While pregnant with Ishmael, Hagar finds herself on the road to Shur, close to Egypt. The "Wilderness of Shur" is the first stop of the Israelites after they cross the Red Sea and also the place where they find only bitter water to drink. Moses purifies the water in the same general location where Hagar met with the angel of Yahweh (by a spring of water).

At this point, it is helpful to see the link between Ishmael, the firstborn of Abraham, and the later descendants of Abraham – Isaac and Jacob. Rather than envisioning perpetual enmity between the two nations, Ishmael can be understood as a prototype of God's firstborn son and Abraham's seed – the children of Israel. Through Moses, God demands that the pharaoh release his firstborn son (Exod 4:22). When the children of Israel are released and flee into the wilderness, they face even greater tribulations. Abraham's son, Ishmael, is also released from slavery by a flight into the wilderness where he, too, faces tribulations. He is protected by God and Hagar, much as the children of Israel were preserved by God for forty years under the leadership of Moses.

These literary points of connection between these two Old Testament characters signal that Hagar was not merely incidental to the story of the exodus. She is, in fact, a prototype of God's deliverance of the Hebrew people. We can think of the Hagar-Ishmael story as the prequel and the Moses-Exodus story as the sequel. The Holy Spirit inspired the story of Hagar and used it as a literary introduction to his Old Testament salvation story – the exodus. The fact of Hagar the Egyptian being a slave to Sarah, the Hebrew matriarch, deepens the plot and signals the reader to take note of the relationship.

This way of reading the Old Testament may be unfamiliar to some of us. Nevertheless, it serves to highlight the complex yet unified tapestry of God's revealed word. The story of God's pursuit of undeserving human beings and the scandalous outpouring of his love is the theme of the exodus. Deuteronomy makes it crystal clear that God is not saving the Hebrew people due to their nobility, beauty, wealth or status, but because it is his nature to show compassion (Deut 7:6–8; 9:4–6). His salvation brings glory to himself and displays his righteousness and love. The story of Hagar and Ishmael is a small thread in the early formation of the tapestry of the Bible. In the exodus, that thread expands to become a major theme of the tapestry. The same thread reappears in the story of Jesus's incarnation and suffering, bringing salvation to his errant creation and reconciling those who were enemies by his cross.

16

Hagar and Ishmael through the Centuries

As we have seen, Hagar is a remarkable woman who encountered the living God in an extraordinary way. Nevertheless, she also poses a problem as she unwittingly becomes a surrogate for Sarai and the means by which Abram and Sarai attempt to secure an heir – a means which God had not appointed. This "wrinkle" in the narrative demonstrates that the Bible has no interest in idealism. Rather than accommodate fairy-tale imaginations, it deals with real life. It is a true account, with twists and turns that may be uncomfortable for those accustomed to storybook happy endings. Hagar shows up as an intrusion in the plotline – an irritant for some, but a significant element of the story that cannot be ignored.

Our discomfort with Hagar arises from other sources as well. The plotline of the Bible brushes her aside, not rudely, but more as a matter of course. She is simply not the central idea it is developing. That central idea comes to fulfillment in Jesus Christ, who comes through the birth line of Isaac. Hagar and Ishmael are marginal characters, even though they receive considerable attention in Genesis. There are many extraneous facts and characters in the Bible so we cope with this complex story by searching for the "big idea." In reading for this "big idea" we naturally tend to overlook Hagar and Ishmael.

Another source of discomfort is the narrative's obvious lack of correspondence to our contemporary values and worldview. Domestic servitude, patriarchy, predefined gender roles and polygamy hardly make for comfortable reading. What's more, the biblical narrative provides no explicit condemnation of these practices despite their obvious destructive effects in family and society. Are we to infer that the Bible condones them, or are we justified in seeing an implicit condemnation through the outcomes?

Finally, as we have already observed, the apostle Paul provided a framework through which to view Hagar and her son. Rather than being overlooked or neglected, Hagar may, in some cases, be vilified. In the absence of a plausible alternative, Paul's analogous interpretation becomes our "go to" option. Would Paul approve of our seeking new insight from the Genesis narrative? Did he intend to forever close the door to a different, expanded, and more generous understanding of Hagar?

What will we do with Hagar? And what of her son, Ishmael?

Before we answer that question, let us consider what our forebears have done with Hagar. After all, we stand on their shoulders as heirs of their thought life.

The history of the Judeo-Christian interpretation of the Hagar story is wide-ranging, yet with some predictability.[1]

In Jewish literature, there are two distinct strains of reflection on Ishmael. One views him as an evil man, unwelcome in the household of the Jewish patriarch. His skill with the bow was employed to shoot at his brother and to conduct raids on unsuspecting travelers.

The second strain views Ishmael as a righteous man, reuniting with his brother in the burial of their father Abraham. One Jewish interpreter surmises that this positive assessment of Ishmael carried some weight through the centuries since a famous second-century Jewish rabbi, often quoted in the Mishnah, was Rabbi Ishmael. It is unlikely indeed that the esteemed rabbi would bear the name of an evil man.[2]

Around the time of Christ, Philo – a Jewish philosopher and scriptural commentator from Alexandria – made popular an allegorical view of Hagar that differed from that of his contemporary, Paul. For Philo, Hagar represented the "preliminary teachings" from which the wise person must graduate in

1. John L. Thompson, "Hagar in Salvation-History: Victim or Villain?," in *Reading the Bible with the Dead: What You Can Learn from the History of Exegesis That You Can't Learn from Exegesis Alone* (Grand Rapids, MI: Eerdmans, 2007). John Thompson has outlined this history in a helpful way. This chapter draws on Thompson's research.

2. Cohen, "Hagar and Ishmael," 255.

order to attain the true wisdom of God represented by Sarah. Hagar is not to be despised, but progress must be made beyond Hagar; otherwise, the wisdom seeker will produce nothing but sophistry – a philosophy that appears valid but is false. This "sophistry" is personified by the son of Hagar – Ishmael.[3]

Philo is important because he influenced other Christian teachers such as Origen, who merged Paul's analogy with that of Philo to explain Abraham's polygamy – a source of some embarrassment for early Christian monogamists. For Origen, Hagar's embodiment of wisdom eliminated the problem of polygamy. Abraham's embrace of a second marriage was the necessary path to his growth in wisdom. Furthermore, Origen saw the Hagar story as God's divine arrangement to set up the analogy of Galatians 4. He gave his allegorical inclinations full vent, proposing that the Jews of his own day were unable to draw the truth of Christ from the Law and the Prophets, just as Hagar was unable to perceive the source of water which lay before her eyes.[4]

A century later, the Western church father Ambrose also picked up on the Philo analogy, but preferred to see in Hagar an example of *worldly* wisdom rather than the necessary "first principles" of wisdom espoused by Philo. He also invoked the Pauline analogy of Galatians 4 to cast Hagar as emblematic of two sources of bondage – the Jewish synagogue and heresy. For Ambrose, the polygamous marriage of Abraham was intended by God to demonstrate how the church would eventually replace the Jewish synagogue. Ambrose's disciple Augustine carried on the same line of thought, perceiving in Hagar a symbol of heresy, particularly the Donatist heresy which was raging in his day.

Certain Jewish rabbis contributed their understanding of Ishmael's "play" with Isaac in Genesis 21, a word which the apostle Paul appears to view as persecution. Though the Hebrew word itself is general, and could express varied nuances, the rabbis linked it with the accusation of Potiphar's wife that Joseph had "made sport" of her. Thus the word was linked with fornication or illicit sexual advances.[5]

Medieval Christian interpretation relied heavily on the allegory of the apostle Paul to associate Jews with the slave woman Hagar, while Sarah – the free woman – represented the church. The discussion extended beyond popular opinion and, at times, became a legal basis for the expulsion of Jews from European lands. The Pauline analogy led to a close association of the

---

3. Thompson, "Hagar in Salvation-History," 18.

4. Deena Klepper, "Historicizing Allegory: The Jew as Hagar in Medieval Christian Text and Image," *Church History* 84.2 (2015): 316.

5. Thompson, "Hagar in Salvation-History," 23.

Jewish people with Hagar in biblical commentary, sermons and art – to such an extent that, from the thirteenth century onwards, Christians increasingly thought of Hagar as the ancestress of the Jewish people![6] This was not the first time, nor the last, that biblical interpretation would be used to buttress racism and prejudice.

The contrast of Christian Isaac with Muslim Ishmael also became a trope of medieval Muslim–Christian polemic, where Isaac was associated with Christians and Ishmael with Muslims. Perhaps the most egregious example is Pope Urban II whose rallying cry for the Crusades was "cast out the slave woman and her son."[7]

In summary, we see that early interpretations of Hagar and Ishmael take a negative trajectory. Hagar, at best, is symbolic of a worldly wisdom that is opposed to God's wisdom. Alternatively, the Hagar–Sarah analogy of Paul is used to foster further animosity towards Jews. In yet more stark terms, Ishmael's antagonism toward Isaac is cast in the worst possible light – sexual harassment. It is difficult to imagine a more disastrous misappropriation of the biblical data on Hagar and Ishmael.

However, not all early interpretations of Hagar were so harsh. Isodore, the seventh-century archbishop of Seville, perceived a precursor of the cross in the tree under which Hagar cast Ishmael in Genesis 21. Hagar's action becomes a pointer to faith and repentance through the cross.

An English monk known as "the Venerable Bede" (d. 735) holds an even more positive view of Hagar, attributing to her remarkable spiritual insight in recognizing and naming the divine person who visited her. His comments move away from the common view of Hagar as representing recalcitrant Jews, and see her as a portent of those – both Jews and others – who would acknowledge Christ's lordship. Raban Maur,[8] an archbishop of Mainz in the ninth century, suggested that Hagar was a type of the Gentile church and a woman who modeled a deep spirituality.

As we move into the period of the Reformation, Luther displays a uniquely positive and empathetic view of Hagar, dwelling at great length on her plight. Her naming of God was a "hymn for the instruction of every one of us" and "an act of true worship." He is deeply concerned by the dilemma of Hagar and Ishmael, and wonders how Abraham could send his wife and son into the wild

---

6. Klepper, "Historicizing Allegory," 310, 319, 344.

7. Thompson, "Hagar in Salvation-History," 29.

8. Raban Maur (or Rabanus Maurus, d. 856) was the archbishop of Mainz in Germany. He was a prolific author in grammar, education and scriptural commentary, and referred to as the "teacher of Germany."

with such meager provisions? Luther writes that "most of us are like Hagar" in that we follow a path from humiliation to repentance. Luther's engagement with Hagar is poignant:

> Surely this is a piteous account, which I can scarcely read with dry eyes, that the mother and son so patiently bear their ejection and wander into exile. And so Father Abraham either stood there weeping, following the wanderers with his blessing and prayers, or else he hid by himself off in a corner, where he cried over his own fate and that of the exiles.[9]

For Luther, Hagar's expulsion felt like being cast off by God himself, a trauma with which Luther was familiar due to the church's rejection of him and his teaching. He rejected the idea that Hagar and Ishmael's expulsion was tantamount to rejection by God, referring to this explanation as a "fabrication of the devil." Abraham is grieved by the desperate fate of his wife and son.[10] God uses such circumstances, as he did in Luther's case, to refine vision and purify faith.[11]

Luther may well have provided the Protestant world an opportunity to reenvision Hagar. Other Reformers, however, were less sympathetic. John Calvin appears to have steered clear of the overly negative view of rabbinic and Christian forebears as well as the empathetic view of his Reformation colleague Martin Luther. Calvin, well-regarded for his objectivity vis-à-vis the biblical text, is reluctant to psychologize a story that provides such scant detail.[12] Although no character in the story remains untarnished in Calvin's commentary, in the main, he follows Augustine and the apostle Paul's analogous interpretation which likens Hagar to the adversaries of faith – which, in his case, were his Roman Catholic opponents. Calvin's approach to Hagar has largely eclipsed that of Luther and remains as an enduring legacy in Protestant thought.

Finally, it is to a Jewish Rabbi that we turn for concluding thoughts on Hagar. Rabbi Jonathan Sacks points to three intriguing passages in the Genesis narrative that lead to a surprising conclusion.[13] The first occurs at the return of Abraham's servant with Rebecca, who is to marry Isaac in Genesis 24:62.

---

9. Quoted in Thompson, "Hagar: Victim or Villain?," 224–226; Thompson, "Hagar in Salvation-History," 25–28, fn 38.

10. Genesis 21:11–14.

11. Thompson, "Hagar: Victim or Villain?," 229; Thompson, "Hagar in Salvation-History," 28.

12. Thompson, "Hagar: Victim or Villain?," 221.

13. Jonathan Sacks, *Covenant and Conversation: A Weekly Reading of the Jewish Bible* (London: Maggid Books, 2009), 141–144.

Isaac comes "from the way of Be'er la-ḥai ro'i." The mention of the place is strange because Abraham resided in Beersheva and Hebron until this point in the narrative. Of course we recognize it as the well that Hagar named, but why does Isaac come from there? The second surprise occurs after Sarah's death. Abraham's love for Sarah through their long journey and many trials together is evident. Nevertheless, Abraham takes another wife after Isaac's marriage. The name of the woman is Keturah by whom Abraham has another six sons. The third surprise is the presence of Ishmael at the burial of Abraham despite his having been banished years earlier (Gen 25:8–10).

Rabbi Sacks relates that the Jewish sages formed a narrative from these three surprising passages as follows. Once Isaac was married, he determined that his father should not live alone while he was comforted by Rebecca. He went to Be'er la-ḥai ro'i in search of Hagar to bring her back to his father. Keturah, then, is actually Hagar. It is not unusual for the ancient people of the Torah to have more than one name. This new name signifies a "fragrance." Thus, our heroine Hagar returns to her husband at the prompting of Isaac. She becomes his wife again in these latter years. As Hagar returns to the house of Abraham, the banishment of Ishmael comes to an end. He joins Isaac in burying his father.

One more detail from Rabbi Sacks's account must be mentioned. An extraordinary midrash in *Pirkei deRabbi Eliezer* relates that after Ishmael's banishment, Abraham went to visit his son twice. He was received hospitably by Ishmael's wife, Fatima, on the second visit. Upon learning that Ishmael was not home, he prayed before departing and as a result Ishmael's house was "filled with all good things." Thus Ishmael came to know of his father's abiding love for him.

The referenced midrash is from the eighth century, the early years of Islam. Ishmael's wife bears the name of the daughter of Muhammad, Fatima, an intentional and positive reference to Islam. The Rabbi's conclusions are worth quoting in full:

> Beneath the surface of the narrative in *Ḥayei Sara*, the sages read the clues and pieced together a moving story of reconciliation between Abraham and Hagar on the one hand, Isaac and Ishmael on the other. Yes, there was conflict and separation; but that was the beginning, not the end. Between Judaism and Islam there can be friendship and mutual respect. Abraham loved both his sons,

and was laid to rest by both. There is hope for the future in this story of the past.[14]

This variegated history of understanding Hagar recalls a sunset on a cloudy day. The dark and foreboding clouds block the sun's light, but not completely. Through openings in the clouds, shafts of light penetrate, illuminating the landscape below. Although the story of Hagar has been largely eclipsed, the pathos and power of the narrative have penetrated at various points in time like great beams of light, revealing the way to a positive and transformative interpretation of the Hagar narrative. In the following chapter, we will allow these shafts of light to suggest how the Hagar story impacts us today.

---

14. Sacks, *Covenant and Conversation*, 144.

17

Hagar Speaks Today

Does Hagar still speak?

In this final chapter, we are confronted with a choice: Will we give Hagar a voice? Does she speak to our world, our society, our generation, to us as individuals?

She is outside the "big idea" in terms of the historical unfolding of God's promise through Abraham. Her biological line is not the focal point of the narrative. Nevertheless, her story testifies to a God who pursues the outcast and restores meaning to our broken and alienated existence.

Hagar is the recipient of two divine revelations. She names the God who encounters her and he names the child in her womb. The scale and intensity of the encounter are exceptional in the biblical narrative, but the quality of the encounter is also extraordinary. The story of Hagar is a gospel encounter. This aspect comes into clear focus as we perceive that the "angel of the LORD" is none other than the preincarnate Christ – the eternal Son of God. His encounter with Hagar is an Old Testament foreshadowing of his meeting with the Samaritan woman – and the outcomes are no less stunning.

Redeemed by grace, Hagar returns with her dignity restored, head held high, her identity now defined in relation to the God who sees her.

Consider a few aspects of her story that commend themselves to the contemporary reader.

First, Hagar confronts us with the uncomfortable reality within us.

The narrative unsettles us. Abraham, the paragon of biblical faith, is passively complicit in Hagar's suffering. Sarah, the matriarch of Israel, is the implement of oppression. Our preconceived notions of moral heroism in these biblical characters are thrown off balance. Glib platitudes will not satisfy if we seriously grapple with this story.

The story confronts the tendency towards self-preservation and aggrandizement which often results in abuse, whether passive or active. We, the "righteous," are forced to examine our lives for the "Hagars" around us. Where are we blind to, or blissfully unaware of, our enmeshment in societal evils that lead, somewhere down the supply chain, to situations of abuse and injustice? Does our consumer lifestyle promote exploitation in developing-world sweat shops? Does our implicit classism contribute to unjust systems which favor the wealthy and disadvantage the poor? Does racism still rear its ugly head as we react to an agent whose language skills are making communication more time-consuming? Much as Hagar's domestic servitude was a normal thread in the societal fabric of Abraham's day, our lifestyle may promote exploitation of some Hagar of whom we are blissfully unaware.

This is not to minimize Hagar's faults, which are woven into the tapestry of the story. She looks down on her mistress, thinking highly of herself as the mother of Abraham's first son. Sarah's sense of significance is deeply wounded and she reacts by wounding her slave girl, who is perceived as the source of her pain. Hagar must be cast out, utterly deprived of a place in the family. Abraham sanctions the exclusion.

Echoes of Christ's teaching to love and bless our enemies and pray for those who persecute us reverberate in the Hagar narrative. Abraham and Sarah, often held up as archetypes of faith, reflect the residual self-centeredness within us even after our initial encounter with Christ. The Hagar story compels us to examine our souls for a self-effacing love of others. Can we rejoice in their good rather than resort to petty self-preservation? Can we trust God even when his favor seems to bypass us and rest on others? The unsettling aspects of the Hagar story challenge us to replace self-love with other-love, to walk the path of death to self in obedient discipleship.

Second, Hagar practices uncomfortable obedience.

Though we courageously cite Jesus's words that those who follow him must deny themselves and take up their cross, we are often at a loss to know what this means in our day-to-day lives. How do we die to self? Is such a thing possible? In our world of self-fulfillment and self-actualization how do we make sense of Jesus's call to discipleship?

The result of Hagar's encounter with Jesus was to return to a place of suffering, servitude, petty rivalries and marginalization. The encounter, we infer, must have been transformative as it was sufficient to displace Hagar's sense of victimization. She had been seen, seen by one of infinite worth, which secured her own worth in his eyes. Her son's name was an enduring testimony of divine attentiveness to her plight.

Hagar models the "expulsive power of a new affection."[1] Her eyes have been lifted from her circumstances. She has seen the beauty of Yahweh and realized that she is the object of his tender care. Though the narrative is sparse in detail, we surmise that her value no longer derives from her role as a domestic servant nor does her dignity lie in bearing Abraham's son. Hagar has entered into relationship with Yahweh himself, which allows her to lay aside the old self. Her new self – a new identity flowing from a new relationship with Yahweh – empowers a new walk.

She returned under Sarah's hand. With the apostle, Hagar would surely testify,

> Who shall separate us from the love of Christ? Shall tribulation, or distress, or persecution, or famine, or nakedness, or danger, or sword? . . . No, in all these things we are more than conquerors through him who loved us. For I am sure that neither death nor life, nor angels nor rulers, nor things present nor things to come, nor powers, nor height nor depth, nor anything else in all creation, will be able to separate us from the love of God in Christ Jesus our Lord. (Rom 8:35, 37–39)

Hagar rebuffs our contemporary fascination with a God who meets all our needs and returns us to the simple beauty of the true God who loves us and gives himself for us.

Third, Hagar holds forth hope of security and acceptance for the outcast and marginalized.

If you are reading these lines, you and I (the author) probably have a lot in common. Our native or second language is likely English and we probably enjoy access to new ideas through various media. We have a respectable education and benefit from a level of personal and ethnic security. We likely fall in the top one percent of the world's population in terms of ownership of material wealth. Our surroundings conspire to hide Hagar from us, but we must remember that she is alive and well in our world.

---

1. This phrase is the title of a sermon by the nineteenth-century Scottish minister and theologian, Thomas Chalmers.

Recent UN statistics indicate a figure of 65 million displaced people around the globe. While media coverage has informed us about the plight of Syrian refugees, many other peoples are desperately seeking refuge, often unnoticed and uncared for. Displaced peoples, refugees and asylum seekers constitute one of the most complex global challenges of our era. How will the church respond? From the Abrahamic blessing (Gen 12:3) to the Great Commission to Paul's unfolding mystery of the inclusion of the Gentiles, the Bible demonstrates that God blesses the nations through his people. When this is embraced as the church's mandate, our attitudes and actions toward the displaced must change.

We can no longer resort to a binary reading of God's blessing and favor. He does not favor one and despise the other. His love embraces Ishmael, securing abundant favor for him though he is outside the line of the promised seed of Abraham.

Given the realities of global displacement and mobility, we can no longer cling to an old mission paradigm of missionaries sent "from the West to the rest." Rather, churches throughout the world must become missional outposts, acting as channels of relief, education, development and gospel reconciliation among all peoples. As the angel of Yahweh encountered Hagar, so the body of Christ, animated by his Spirit, encounters and embraces the refugee in flight today. Hagar powerfully reminds us that God has ample blessing for all. Her story can inspire us to find promise and potential in this fleeing horde of refugees.

As the angel of Yahweh poses two penetrating questions to the slave girl, might we too enter into empathetic and life-giving relationships with new neighbors who have been deprived of their home of origin? The reception they receive in Christ's church can do much to uphold their dignity and honor amid great upheaval and trauma. Today's Hagar can still encounter, and indeed must encounter, Yahweh through the body of Christ, animated by his Spirit and ministering through his resurrection power.

Fourth, Hagar and Ishmael inspire us to reconsider their progeny – the Arab people.

Arabs have become associated with Islam, though we must remember that many Arabs are not Muslims. We will consider this association further in an appendix, but suffice to say that Muhammad, the prophet of Islam, is thought to be the descendant of Abraham through Ishmael. Though the religion of Islam encompasses many diverse peoples and ethnic groups, the association still stands in our minds as well as being the self-perception of Muslims. Arabs are often referred to as the "sons of Ishmael."

Further complicating matters, Islam, rightly or wrongly, is associated in our day with "Islamic terror." A tirade of media monikers instantly comes to mind: 9/11, al-Qaeda, ISIS, al-Nusra Front, Hamas, Hezbollah, Islamic Jihad, terms that have entered our everyday language as pressure points in a world gone mad.

Much of the political rhetoric we hear is directed at these organizations. Fear has engulfed the Western world as terror attacks from Madrid to London to Paris to New York to Los Angeles have proliferated. Frustration and chaos spread through the non-Western world as Islamic militants seek to assert their presence and authority in diverse locations including Syria, Iraq, Yemen, Saudi Arabia, Pakistan and Indonesia. Small wonder that the legacy of enmity and hostility continues to be laid at the feet of Ishmael.

It is important to realize that, no matter how much the media magnify these terror organizations, they represent a very small percentage of Muslims worldwide and that, in fact, the Islamic world *en masse* resists these militant expressions, calling for peaceful coexistence in a world increasingly characterized by diversity.

Even prior to the advent of Islamic militancy, Muslims were often described by Christian spokespersons as the "most resistant" people to the gospel of Christ, and with good reason. Nevertheless, new winds are blowing in the Muslim world. Current research indicates a surprising openness to Christ's gospel among Muslim people groups.[2] One of the most surprising aspects of the massive displacement from Muslim countries due to ISIS and its counterparts is the openness of many Muslims to examining the claims of Christ in their new settings characterized by greater freedom of thought and expression.

Jesus also dealt with an ethnic and religious group perceived by his Jewish contemporaries as their staunch enemy, who had corrupted their holy books, polluted their holy bloodline, and moved their holy sites – the Samaritans. Suffice to say that the clash, not unlike the current conflicts between Western powers and Muslim militants, escalated to armed conflict. It is in this atmosphere of crippling fear and enmity that Jesus chooses to go through Samaria on his way to Jerusalem.

The details are well-known. He engages a Samaritan woman by the well. Her scandalous liaisons pose no obstacle to him. He dismisses the disciples' plea that he eat, preferring the food of doing his Father's will. He seems to genuinely delight in his dialogue with this woman and her co-religionists.

---

2. See David Garrison, *Wind in the House of Islam* (Monument, CO: WIGTake Resources, 2014).

He even prophesies that the disciples will be sent to reap where they had not sown; subsequently, they do reap a great harvest among the Samaritans as a result of Philip's evangelistic ministry there.[3]

The final rejoinder of Jesus to his disciples stands as a towering rebuke to their failure to break free of their cultural blinders: "Look, I tell you, lift up your eyes, and see that the fields are white for harvest."[4] This is new perspective at its best! Paradigm shift. Transformative vision. Call it what you will – it beckons the disciples to a profound missional reorientation.

If Jesus were among us today, he would do no less. It is part and parcel of his call to discipleship to challenge the way we view the world and call us to embrace his higher purposes against the cultural current of fear and exclusion.

Hagar and Ishmael represent a biblical seed whereby our perception of Arab and Muslim peoples can be transformed if we are willing to lift up our eyes, to change our perspective.

God's "seeing" of Hagar and the destiny he promised her – that through her son he would break the yoke of bondage – should give us pause and prompt us to recalibrate our preconceived notions about Muslims. The inclusion of Ishmael in God's covenant symbolized by circumcision should invigorate our hope that many Arabs and Muslims will find their peace with God in the promised seed of Abraham – Jesus.

Indeed, there are indicators that "a little cloud like a man's hand"[5] is appearing as many of Ishmael's sons and Hagar's daughters are finding freedom as joyful disciples of Jesus.

So Hagar, the little servant girl from Egypt, packs a powerful punch if we are willing to plumb the depths of God's word, allowing it to transform our thoughts and actions.

Are we willing?

---

3. Acts 8:4–8.
4. John 4:35b.
5. 1 Kings 18:44 .

Appendix

Ishmael: Father of the Arabs?

What are the historic roots of the association of Ishmael with the Arab peoples and specifically with the religion of Islam? Is this association factual or mythical or something between the two?

Most of what is known of the life of Muhammad is taken from his biography, which was penned years after his death. The biography traces his line of descent to Abraham through Ishmael.[1] As we will see below, the direct links are not as certain as the Islamic sources would have us believe. Nevertheless, the association remains an article of faith for most Muslims. Even Muslims who are not well-read in the Islamic source materials are generally aware that Ishmael was the son of Abraham through whom Muhammad traces his descent.

The Qur'an mentions Ishmael several times, including his name in lists citing the patriarchs as prophets.[2] What is surprising to readers of the Hebrew scripture (the Old Testament) is the prevailing Muslim view that Abraham's sacrifice of his son took place in Mecca, Saudi Arabia. If that were not sufficiently problematic, Abraham's attempted sacrifice, which the angel intervened to halt, was not of Isaac, but of Ishmael. Although this is not stated

---

1. Ibn Ishaq, *The Life of Muhammad*, trans. Alfred Guillaume (Karachi: Oxford University Press, 1995), 3–4. The biography was written by Ibn Ishaq at least 120 years after Muhammad's death and edited by Ibn Hisham more than 200 years after Muhammad. The work remains as the most reliable representative of Ibn Ishaq's work. Due to its lack of historical proximity to Muhammad, many critical scholars are reluctant to accept its testimony. Muslim scholars have noted abnormalities as well. Another Islamic historian and scholar named al-Tabari also wrote a history of Muhammad's life. His primary source was Ibn Ishaq's work. Therefore al-Tabari provides a second source for critical comparison with Ibn Hisham's edition.

2. Qur'an 2:136, 140; 3:84; 4:163. The order is "Abraham, Ishmael, Isaac and Jacob."

113

explicitly in the Qur'an, it is generally held by Qur'anic commentators, with some notable exceptions.

The shift of location from Paran to Mecca is fully integrated into Islamic lore by the eighth-century biography of Muhammad. The narrative tells of Abraham departing Syria, led by the shekinah wind with whom the patriarch conversed. Upon arrival in Mecca, Abraham is instructed to build a temple with his son, Ishmael. Thus the Kaaba – the rectangular structure which serves as the focal point of the Muslim pilgrimage – is attributed to Abraham and Ishmael.[3]

The Islamic Hadith (the collected traditions of Muhammad) depicts Ishmael and his mother in the area of Mecca, roughly 600 miles to the south of the region of Paran. Hagar's provision of water is said to have come from the well of Zamzam, after she ran a circuit between the hills of Safa and Marwah seven times as she anxiously sought a water source for her son. Muslim pilgrims still run this circuit and drink from the Zamzam well in Mecca, commemorating Hagar's desert plight. If nothing else, the continual reenactment of the Hagar and Ishmael story by modern-day Muslim pilgrims demonstrates how deeply Islamic history and piety draws on the story. Ishmael is counted among the patriarchs and is also a prophet – meaning that he received a revelation from God.

Nevertheless, this geographic shift to the south in Islamic sources finds no support in the Hebrew Bible, which locates Ishmael and Hagar in Paran (Gen 21:21), in the northeast of the Sinai Peninsula. Later, his family settles from Havilah to Shur (Gen 25:18) – an area stretching from the coast of Egypt to the northwest of the Sinai or possibly the west coast of Arabia.[4]

Beyond questions of geography, the Old Testament helpfully provides a wider lens through which to view the peoples of the Middle East. Noah's sons were Shem, Ham and Japheth. Shem became the father of the Semites – a broad grouping of Middle Eastern peoples. Shem's descendant was Eber, who had two sons, Peleg and Joktan, and Joktan's descendants populated the Arabian Peninsula well before the time of Abraham.[5]

Doubtless, there were other streams that fed into the conglomeration of peoples of the Middle East. Therefore it is inaccurate to assume that all those

---

3. Klepper, "Historicizing Allegory," 314–315.

4. Colin Chapman, "Second Thoughts about the Ishmael Theme," *Seedbed* 4, no. 4: 52.

5. Genesis 10:30 mentions that the descendants of Joktan lived in an area from "Mesha in the direction of Sephar to the hill country of the east." Although these place names are difficult to identify, Mesha is thought to be located in the north of the Arabian Peninsula and Sephar in the south. K. A. Matthews, *Genesis 1–11:26*, NAC Logos Edition (Nashville: Broadman & Holman, 2005), 465.

living in the Arabian Peninsula were direct descendants of Ishmael – whether in the days of the Bible or in the subsequent period which witnessed the birth of Islam. Muhammad's descent from Ishmael is an article of faith, asserted by Muslim texts even though it cannot be proven by independent sources.

The Christians of the Middle East, who encountered the Islamic invasions of the seventh century shortly after the death of Muhammad, used biblical monikers to describe their invaders. John of Damascus (d. 743) provides the etymology. The Muslims were portrayed as Hagarenes because they were born of Hagar; or as Saracens for their having been cast out by Sarah; or as Ishmaelites.[6]

If we fast forward a few thousand years to our day, identifying a single source of biological descent for the Arab peoples is impossible. If we limit our study to the Arabian Peninsula we have the issue of wars and intermarriage resulting in genetic variations. Even Ishmael married an Egyptian according to the Bible.

Usually, however, when we speak of "Arabs" today, we are referring to the peoples whose native language is Arabic, spread across twenty-two nations from Morocco to Iraq, from Syria to Djibouti. When understood in this contemporary sense, the designation "Arab" includes a vast array of peoples including Phoenicians, Pharaonic Egyptians, Amazigh Berbers, Nubians, Kurds, African tribal peoples and many others. It also includes several million Christians of many denominations, Druze, Alawites, Mandaeans, Jews, Bahai, and people of other religious faiths and no religious faith.

Again, it is an inaccurate generalization to refer to Arabs as the descendants of Ishmael, particularly if we intend to refer to "speakers of Arabic" from the twenty-two Arab nations.

However, if we take a step back from critical historiography and birthlines determined by DNA, we realize that the fatherhood of Ishmael has enormous symbolic significance for the Arab peoples. He is their link to Abraham, the father of the faithful and the original worshiper of the one God.

This is not unlike the Christian concept of Abraham's fatherhood. Followers of Christ share the faith of Abraham, though it has nothing to do with biological descent. In fact, Jesus's disciples, following the apostle Paul, hold that true sonship to Abraham comes through the faith of Abraham. Even Jesus rebuked his contemporaries by pointing out that if Abraham were their father, they should be acting like Abraham. Their behavior (plotting to kill Jesus) demonstrated their disassociation from Abraham.

---

6. Klepper, "Historicizing Allegory," 318.

By acknowledging the symbolic and spiritual association of Arabs with Ishmael, we honor their spiritual identity and create a bond of kinship. Furthermore, as we realize God's intention to bless and sustain Ishmael, our prayers and hopes for Arab and Muslim peoples are given new life.

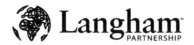

Langham Literature and its imprints are a ministry of Langham Partnership.

Langham Partnership is a global fellowship working in pursuit of the vision God entrusted to its founder John Stott –

to facilitate the growth of the church in maturity and Christ-likeness through raising the standards of biblical preaching and teaching.

Our vision is to see churches in the majority world equipped for mission and growing to maturity in Christ through the ministry of pastors and leaders who believe, teach and live by the Word of God.

Our mission is to strengthen the ministry of the Word of God through:
- nurturing national movements for biblical preaching
- fostering the creation and distribution of evangelical literature
- enhancing evangelical theological education

especially in countries where churches are under-resourced.

Our ministry

Langham Preaching partners with national leaders to nurture indigenous biblical preaching movements for pastors and lay preachers all around the world. With the support of a team of trainers from many countries, a multi-level programme of seminars provides practical training, and is followed by a programme for training local facilitators. Local preachers' groups and national and regional networks ensure continuity and ongoing development, seeking to build vigorous movements committed to Bible exposition.

Langham Literature provides majority world preachers, scholars and seminary libraries with evangelical books and electronic resources through publishing and distribution, grants and discounts. The programme also fosters the creation of indigenous evangelical books in many languages, through writer's grants, strengthening local evangelical publishing houses, and investment in major regional literature projects, such as one volume Bible commentaries like *The Africa Bible Commentary* and *The South Asia Bible Commentary*.

Langham Scholars provides financial support for evangelical doctoral students from the majority world so that, when they return home, they may train pastors and other Christian leaders with sound, biblical and theological teaching. This programme equips those who equip others. Langham Scholars also works in partnership with majority world seminaries in strengthening evangelical theological education. A growing number of Langham Scholars study in high quality doctoral programmes in the majority world itself. As well as teaching the next generation of pastors, graduated Langham Scholars exercise significant influence through their writing and leadership.

To learn more about Langham Partnership and the work we do visit **langham.org**

Lightning Source UK Ltd.
Milton Keynes UK
UKHW011402171019

351785UK00010B/232/P